Literary L.A.

9/5/81
For David & Janet Peoples:
Two very dear friends who
write... sometimes in L.A.
Mikhe

Litera

ry L.A.

LIONEL ROLFE

CHRONICLE

BOOKS

SAN FRANCISCO

*This book is dedicated to my wife, Nigey Lennon Rolfe,
who oftentimes believed in it more than I did.
And Dick Adler surely should be acknowledged for first
pointing out to me that I was writing a book.*

PHOTO CREDITS
Mark Twain, Theodore Dreiser, Henry Miller, and
Thomas Mann: The Bettman Archive, Inc. Malcolm
Lowry, Aldous Huxley: San Francisco *Chronicle* Library.
Laura and Aldous Huxley: photograph by Rosenys.
Nathanael West: photograph, "West in 1931, the year *The
Dream Life of Balso Snell* was published," from
Nathanael West: The Art of His Life by Jay Martin,
copyright © 1970 by Jay Martin, reprinted by permission of
Farrar, Straus & Giroux, Inc. Jack London and George
Sterling: reprinted from *The Seacoast of Bohemia* by
Franklin Walker, copyright © 1966 by The Book Club of
California, all rights reserved, reproduced by permission.
Bas-relief of Jack London: photograph by Phil Stern.
Robinson and Una Jeffers: Jeffers Collection,
Library, California State University, Long Beach. Upton
Sinclair: photograph by John Dreyer.

THE AUTHOR WISHES TO ACKNOWLEDGE
the sources of material quoted: "The Answer," copyright
© 1937 and renewed 1965 by Donnan Jeffers and Garth
Jeffers, reprinted from *The Selected Poetry of
Robinson Jeffers* by permission of Random House, Inc.
Passage from *Dark As the Grave Wherein My Friend Is
Laid* by Malcolm Lowry, and Malcolm Lowry epitaph,
copyright © 1968 and copyright © 1973 by Margerie Bonner
Lowry, reprinted by permission of Literistic, Ltd.

LIBRARY OF CONGRESS CATALOGING IN PUBLICATION DATA
Rolfe, Lionel, 1942–
Literary L.A.
Bibliography: p. 99
1. American literature—California—Los Angeles—History
and criticism. 2. American literature—20th
century—History and criticism. 3. Authors, American—
California—Los Angeles—Biography. 4. Bohemianism—
California—Los Angeles. 5. Los Angeles (Calif.)—
Intellectual life. I. Title.
PS285.L7R6   810'.9'979493   81-4867
ISBN 0-87701-177-X   AACR2

PORTIONS OF THIS BOOK
were excerpted in the Los Angeles *Herald-Examiner.*

EDITING BY HARPER AND VANDENBURGH
DESIGN AND TYPOGRAPHY BY HOWARD JACOBSEN
COVER PHOTOGRAPH BY ROSENYS
HAND-COLORING BY CHARLES MIZE

CHRONICLE BOOKS
870 Market Street · San Francisco, California 94102

AN ILLUSTRATED CONTENTS

Mark Twain

Henry Miller

Theodore Dreiser

Nathanael West

Malcolm Lowry

Aldous Huxley (above);
Thomas Mann (far left);
Jack London and George
Sterling (left)

Robinson and Una Jeffers (below); Upton Sinclair (right)

PREFACE

No one has yet precisely pinpointed the literary tradition of Los Angeles; but then, L.A. itself is a hard place to pinpoint. Perhaps this is because L.A. became a major city of the world without having had a history that went back for centuries. From its relatively recent beginnings, Los Angeles has been a magnet for the Bohemians—the gypsies and wanderers—of our culture, and of other cultures. We are a city of refugees and displaced persons, of modern mobile American corporation workers, and we have achieved, at least in appearance, a certain homogenous quality, perhaps hoping that it will make up for the roots we lack. The transitory aspects of the contemporary human condition have been institutionalized in Los Angeles, and the face of this madness and uncertainty can be glimpsed in some of the writings that have come out of this city.

I was reared in a European home-in-exile in Los Angeles, a home where the chief concerns were cultural and intellectual. There were elements of Bohemia in my mother Yaltah—although there was a sterner tradition operating in my family as well, which I wrote about in my first book, *The Menuhins: A Family Odyssey*—and my reading had drawn me to the California Bohemians without my even being aware that this was happening. But the closest approximations I found to Bohemians in Los Angeles were the Beatniks and intellectuals of the coffeehouse movement that was in vogue then, during the 1950s and '60s. I was

drawn to them because they were quite conscious of the fact the Bohemians were their ancestors. The other intellectuals and wanderers of my acquaintance were Aldous Huxley and Thomas Mann, members of the Holocaust generation of writers whose stories form the first part of this book. The last half of the book, where we get back to the roots of Los Angeles's literary tradition, concerns itself with members of the California Bohemians.

The one obvious characteristic that unites these two generations of writers is the modern condition of rootlessness. Hollywood has undoubtedly contributed much to the transitory and illusory quality that shines through in the best writing involving Los Angeles. But even without a Hollywood, L.A. might have fostered a literature of the brief encounter, the momentary assignation that sometimes ends up in seduction. The truth is that the rootlessness of the place may have been an aberration of history, but Los Angeles has turned that aberration into a powerful kind of adaptive mechanism. Ebb and flow, a non-homogenous collection of human types piled decades high upon the magnificent California landscape had to produce something distinctive, something different than the writing that issued from New York and Europe. What it produced was a hidden literary tradition in Los Angeles, which this book will be devoted to ferreting out.

[LOS ANGELES, CALIFORNIA · JANUARY 1981]

ONE

Just Passing Through

THE GHOSTS OF TWAIN, DREISER, STEINBECK, MILLER, KEROUAC AND OTHERS

L *os Angeles is a town of never-ending motion—rootless, transitory. Here today, gone tomorrow. But passing through, not permanence, has become a major part of the human condition in the twentieth century. They say that if you turn America on its end, everything loose slides into L.A.; well, a few of our great literary artists happened by, too, and commenced writing major works before moving on.*

I first became intrigued with the idea of writers "just passing through" years ago, when I was caught up in a minor mystery surrounding one of the greatest and most truly American of American writers,

Mark Twain. Back in the late '6os when I went to work as a reporter on the *Newhall Signal,* one of the first persons I met was the town historian, Arthur B. Perkins. Newhall is only thirty-five miles north of Los Angeles City Hall, and it is beginning to look more and more like any L.A. suburb, but it still has some of the feeling of an old western town. Perkins had his office in the back of the Chamber of Commerce, which was located right across the courtyard from the *Newhall Signal.* On hot summer days when things got slow and everyone kept the doors open so the stale air would circulate better, I got in the habit of wandering across the courtyard and through Perkins's open door. Perkins was still tall and imposing and only a little shaky for a man in his nineties. For a young reporter trying to learn all about a town during his first weeks on the job, Perkins was a wonderful find. His cussedness and literate intelligence somehow branded him as the old New Englander he actually was, but it also seemed as if he had lived in Newhall forever. There was hardly a thing in the town's history that he hadn't meticulously researched.

I never forgot his telling, one afternoon, how Samuel Clemens (also known as Mark Twain) had come to Newhall in the 186os. The stagecoach stop in Newhall then was called Lyon's Station, and Twain was coming to visit nearby Placerita Canyon, where in 1842 a Franciscan friar named Don Francisco Lopez had, in the course of plucking some wild onions while sitting under an oak tree, discovered flecks of placer gold on the roots. California gold, contrary to what is generally thought, was not first discovered at Sutter's Mill near Sacramento in 1848, but rather in Placerita Canyon. (That oak was later officially described and commemorated as "The Oak of the Golden Dreams.") By the 186os there were regular commercial mining operations going on. And not far away, in Pico Canyon, oil seeping through the ground was being used to keep the lights burning in the San Fernando Mission.

Recently I checked Perkins's thoughts on Mark Twain with Ruth and Tony Newhall of the Newhall family who ran the newspaper then, and neither of them could verify the Twain story. But I was able to find a long piece by Perkins that the Southern Historical Society had published in 1958. If Twain did come to Newhall, Perkins apparently discovered it after he wrote that article, which was entitled "Mining Camps of the Soledad."

I was perhaps too eager to place Twain in the same town I was starting out to cover. I would have dropped the notion forever but for the fact that over the years a former coffeehouse entrepreneur, sometime journalist, poet, and title searcher in downtown Los Angeles — Walden "Monty" Muns — kept telling me about the strange old 330 N. Broadway Building. It was replaced by a parking structure several years ago, but if it were still standing it would be located next to the Hall of Justice. Muns's job took him into the building almost daily, for the place was used as a repository for records of probate cases. One day Muns asked the veteran clerk there why the building had so many strange, narrow stairways, cubby-holes, and private rooms. The clerk replied that the building had been a "hotel" at the turn of the century. More specifically, it had been a whorehouse. Mark Twain was once a regular patron of the establishment and even had his own room there, the old clerk contended. Other regulars, he added, were Hart Crane and Bret Harte.

I can't vouch for the accuracy of the yarn about Mark Twain in Los Angeles, but it *is* true that there has been a curiously unexamined relationship between a surprising number of great writers and the City of the Angels. While New York has maintained a persuasive claim to being the nation's literary capital, it was in California that the frontier character of this country found its most expressive voice. The frontier influence was eloquent and rough-hewn; New York felt uncomfortable in its presence. In the aftermath of the San Francisco gold rush, men of letters didn't turn to New York for guidance; they were much more influenced by the Paris Bohemians of the 1840s. During his California days, Mark Twain was known by his San Francisco newspaper colleagues, not always affectionately, as the "Sagebrush Bohemian."

After the 1906 earthquake, the Bohemian community was forced to abandon San Francisco. Some moved to Carmel, which became the nucleus of a flourishing literary scene that included such giants of American literature as Ambrose Bierce, Jack London, Sinclair Lewis, Theodore Dreiser, Upton Sinclair, Lincoln Steffens, Robinson Jeffers, and—only a little less directly—John Steinbeck, and finally, the King of the Beats, Jack Kerouac. At the same time, the emerging city of the south—Los Angeles—was becoming a part of the circuit of the wandering Bohemians.

The Carmel colony was founded shortly before the 1906 earthquake by George Sterling and Mary Austin, minor writers but not minor characters. Sterling was a close friend and champion of a great many important writers. Mary Austin authored some thirty-five books in her lifetime, and was often compared with her friend (and my godmother) Willa Cather. Sinclair Lewis's female protagonist in *Main Street* had her origins in Austin's *A Woman of Genius,* and Theodore Dreiser's *The Genius* also owed a debt to the Austin volume. In her day she was regarded as an intellectual heavyweight. Before going to Carmel she had been part of the literary circle around Charles F. Lummis, who was, among other things, Los Angeles City Librarian. (He was also a great entertainer of artists and intellectuals from all over the world. His adobe house—on the Arroyo between Pasadena and Los Angeles—is a state monument today.) The only book of Mary Austin's which you'll find in most libraries now is *The Land of Little Rain,* written about the

mountains and deserts that form the northern boundaries of the Los Angeles basin. Austin left the region in 1903 and avoided returning to Los Angeles. She had developed a strong distaste for L.A., in part because of the way in which the City of the Angels stole the water from the Owens River Valley on the east side of the Sierra Nevada, where she had lived for some years.

In the Victorian age, the Bohemians were the apostles of hedonism of all kinds, known for their unconventional behavior in matters of sex, inebriation, and general good times. An underlying aspect of the Bohemians, however, was their social conscience. Even the very conservative Ambrose Bierce, who rejected the Carmel colony as a "bunch of anarchists," was a marvelous social critic, and his outrageous cynicism was put to this use in such works as *The Devil's Dictionary.*

The Bohemians were not always the soul of consistency—neither was their godfather Mark Twain, for that matter. Some were revolutionary socialists; others were unreconstructed reactionaries. Most, however, were irreligious and disreputable, at least in the eyes of their contemporary society. A surprising number seem to have died as a result of suicide. Yet a few were mystics and puritans, and many were concerned with nature and made it the motif of much of their work.

An important writer in George Sterling's charmed circle was Theodore Dreiser. When Dreiser came to Los Angeles for a three-year stay in 1919, he had not yet written his most famous and successful work, *An American Tragedy.* Dreiser was living with his cousin and companion of many years, Helen Richardson, whom he didn't make Mrs. Dreiser until the end of his life. About midway through their L.A. stay, Dreiser and Richardson went north to meet Sterling. Being like-minded rebels and pessimists, Sterling and Dreiser quickly took to each other. Sterling also took to Helen, whom he amused by taking off his clothes and swimming into a lake to retrieve some dripping water lilies.

Born in 1871 in Terre Haute, Indiana, Dreiser was as well known for being the brother of songwriter and Tin Pan Alley mogul Paul Dreiser—for whom he wrote the lyrics to the song, "On the Banks of the Wabash"—as for his novel, *Sister Carrie*. *Sister Carrie* had been a controversial book when it was published in 1900, and hadn't done well. Dreiser was an extreme mechanist who thought that everything was determined by biology and environment. He wrote in a hard, cheaply journalistic style at times, for he had made his daily living as a newspaper and magazine writer. In recent years Dreiser has fallen out of favor with American critics and readers, but the scope of his storytelling and his unremitting realism gave him a place in America's literary pantheon which no one can take away.

Nonetheless, his life was often messy. When Dreiser left Gotham to come to L.A. in 1919, he was doing so to avoid his wife (from whom he was separated) as well as publishers anxious to know how his writing— for which they had advanced him money and then seen very little—was going. Dreiser wouldn't even give his close friend H.L. Mencken anything more than a post office box in Los Angeles. At first he and Helen lived in a rented part of a private home on Alvarado Street. After that, according to W.A. Swanberg's biography, *Dreiser,* the couple moved often. They lived in a bungalow on Sunset Boulevard and a cottage in Glendale. Helen, an actress, was speculating in real estate, like almost everyone else. Mencken despaired of ever seeing his friend again. He wrote, "Dreiser is in Los Angeles. What he is doing there I don't know. I have heard that he is being kept by some rich wench."

In fact, Helen was not doing all that badly. She had a couple of supporting acting roles, including one in Rudolph Valentino's first flick, *The Four Horsemen of the Apocalypse*. Dreiser seemed bored and resentful of her success. He called L.A. "the city of the folded hands." He was flagrantly unfaithful to Helen. After three years in L.A. Dreiser was convinced that the city was no place for an artist. He had, however, put aside *The Bulwark* and tentatively begun *An American Tragedy,* his big book.

When he returned to New York, with Helen abandoning her career to follow him, he finished *An American Tragedy,* but then had a long fallow period. By 1935 he wanted to go back to L.A. again. He had a close friend, George Douglas, who worked on the *Los Angeles Examiner*. He moved in with Douglas, and Helen rented a room nearby. After a while, Dreiser and Helen rented an apartment on Rosewood and moved in together again. They didn't stay there long, however: they returned to New York. Dreiser wanted to go back to Los Angeles the following year, but Douglas had died. It wasn't until 1939 that Dreiser and Helen got back together and moved permanently to L.A., taking an apartment at 253-A West Loraine Street in Glendale.

The second time Dreiser made Los Angeles his home it did not help him out of his fallow period. He continued working on *The Bulwark* and *The Stoic,* books that dated way back in his career. But the going was rough, and both books were only published after Dreiser's death here in 1945. Los Angeles had helped him out of a bind once before, but Dreiser and Helen were not living well at the beginning of the second L.A. years. For a while they had an apartment at 1426 North Hayworth, just off Sunset Boulevard. Dreiser was so ashamed of the place that when his old friend Sherwood Anderson came to town, Dreiser didn't bring him back to the apartment. He took Anderson out to eat in a restaurant near the Figueroa Hotel. Later, things improved a bit; the couple moved to a place they had purchased at 1015 N. Kings Road, near Santa Monica Boulevard, and they added a new couple to their social life—Charles and Oona Chaplin, who also were good friends of Upton and Mary Sinclair.

Dreiser, however, suffered from deep intellectual confusions. One day he drove out to Torrance to consult a fortuneteller. Another evening he and Helen went to a seance in Pasadena at the home of the Sinclairs. The political conflicts of the day inflamed him: he was as bothered by corruption in City Hall as he was by the bad news from the Spanish Civil War. On the one hand he became a member of the Communist Party; at the same time, like such other mystics as Aldous Huxley and Christopher Isherwood, he was serious about yoga and contemplated a trip to India. He was no longer able to produce a single, powerful vision of things. Perhaps this was because he wasn't a twentieth-century writer so much as he was a writer who bridged the two centuries. And perhaps it was because he was such a Bohemian.

Usually when people talk about Bohemian writers in Los Angeles, they think of the Garden of Allah, where F. Scott Fitzgerald, Robert Benchley, and Dorothy Parker drank and partied and lived through some of the Depression years while earning fabulous salaries from the nearby Hollywood dream factories. Writers like Somerset Maugham, Dashiell Hammett, and S.J. Perelman were frequent visitors to the Garden of Allah. Hemingway met Gary Cooper there, and they became great friends. Had he been around in those days, Mark Twain could easily have been the king of the roost there, for Hollywood was attracting people from all over with its own kind of gold rush: a celluloid rush. But Twain, of course, was dead by then, and the Garden of Allah is no longer to be seen, except as a model display on the grounds of the savings and loan that displaced the famed residence-hotel at the corners of Sunset and Laurel Canyon boulevards.

Twain would probably have been uncomfortable at the Garden of Allah anyway, since it was primarily a hangout for Eastern writers who regarded the natives as baboons and yahoos. This Eastern chauvinism would not have been Twain's cup of tea at all, although oddly enough the worst of the Eastern chauvinists was the most Bohemian of the writers there, Dorothy Parker. Parker, in fact, was the most Twain-like of the group. She was a great wit, the star of the famed Algonquin Hotel group from the '20s in New York City. In retrospect, it appears that her greatness as a writer was underestimated because of her wit, and this also happened to Twain. Parker left no novels; her output was comprised mainly of literary essays, short stories, and very quotable and funny poetry. Yet those short works, which have been reissued by Viking Press as *The Portable Dorothy Parker,* show that her writing compared favorably with Hemingway's. Despite this, it seems as if her reputation will forever record her as originator of the line, "Men don't make passes at girls who wear glasses." At her husband's funeral, when an aquaintance asked her if she needed anything, she snapped, "Yes. You can get me another husband." The acquaintance was shocked, and asked Dorothy Parker if she really had meant that. Parker's reply: "Then get me a ham sandwich and hold the mustard."

Her wit was as quick against her friends as it was against her enemies. She lived much of her life in a New York Bohemian milieu, and many of her friends were undoubtedly "authors and actors and artists and such." Yet in her poem "Bohemia" she wails that "People Who Do Things exceed my endurance; God, for a man that solicits insurance."

To Dorothy Parker, Hollywood was a zoo in which she happened to have lived for nearly two full decades, off and on. She regarded her bosses in the studios as cretins, which they probably were, so she had funny things to say about Hollywood. And very true things. But the Garden of Allah was more interesting than important in Los Angeles's literary tradition.

In 1976 Tom Dardis wrote *Some Time In the Sun,* which put forth the revisionist theory that ultimately

Hollywood didn't do so badly by people like Fitzgerald, Faulkner, West, and Huxley. He also noted that these and other writers made their contribution to Hollywood in such classic films as *The Big Sleep, Jane Eyre, The African Queen, To Have and Have Not* and *Pride and Prejudice."*

Dardis argued that Hollywood aided these men financially and creatively. His argument about Fitzgerald is worth considering. Fitzgerald's last years in Hollywood were not as bad as they have been portrayed, Dardis maintains. Fitzgerald's reputation and creative powers had plummeted by the middle of the Depression and it was only after he had come to Hollywood that he finally found "something new to write about." *The Last Tycoon* was his California book, and his publishers were every bit as excited by it as they had been during his glorious days in the '20s. Dardis does not deny that Fitzgerald was drinking, but even that has been exaggerated, he argues.

Dardis says that the "ultimate source for all these 'ruined, shattered man' descriptions" of Fitzgerald was Budd Schulberg, of *What Makes Sammy Run?* fame. Schulberg had worked with Fitzgerald on movie jobs, and had drunk with him; Fitzgerald had also recommended Shulberg's book to Random House. But Fitzgerald did not think that Schulberg was talented, and Dardis suggest the latter might thus have had some motivation to paint Fitzgerald as a failure.

To my mind, Dardis is a little less convincing in the case of William Faulkner. Over a period of time Faulkner spent more than four years in Hollywood. His best known effort on a script was *The Big Sleep,* and his main influence here seemed to be the addition of a Southern feeling to a Southern California setting. Considering that a good part of L.A.'s population emigrated from the South, he might have been onto something. Faulkner, however, did not take his writing duties in Hollywood as seriously as did Fitzgerald, for example. He wasn't paid as well, either. He couldn't afford to stay at the Garden of Allah, so the great Faulkner lived in shabby hotels and took long, solitary walks on downtown L.A.'s grubby streets. And he drank like crazy, for he wanted to go home to Oxford, Mississippi. Dardis argues, however, that ultimately the Hollywood money enabled Faulkner to write his great books, and that the Hollywood influence is to be seen in some of them.

Then there was the case of Evelyn Waugh, who spent a short while in Los Angeles and went back to England to write *The Loved One.* Dardis didn't write about him, but we will here. Waugh was a rather typical English gentleman who took his Church of England background so seriously that he later converted to Catholicism. On his short visit to the City of the Angels, what he was most taken with was the L.A. way of death, at least as it was represented by Forest Lawn. As one Waugh biographer put it, *The Loved One* was a satire on "the decline of religious belief and practice in the twentieth century, as evidenced in the California burial customs Waugh had observed while in Hollywood." Waugh was also writing about the English-in-exile in Hollywood. To my mind *The Loved One* is a rather good book, but falls short of being a major contribution to literary Los Angeles. It's been suggested that Aldous Huxley did a better job on the themes of death and California in his *After Many A Summer Dies The Swan.*

It was not the muse of the movies that drew John Steinbeck to Southern California at the nadir of the Great Depression. Steinbeck was not yet a successful writer when he moved to the L.A. area at the beginning of 1930. But not too many years later, he would don the mantle of the great California writer with such books as *Tortilla Flat, Grapes of Wrath,* and *Cannery Row.* Steinbeck grew up in the Carmel-Salinas area, which became known as "Steinbeck country." Yet at a point in his life, perhaps when he was still looking for the muse, he moved south.

His novel *Cannery Row* is about Monterey, but there is a chapter in it about Tom and Mary Talbot, a writer and his wife, which was actually based on two periods of Steinbeck's life when he had moved away from the Northern California coastal region in which he grew up.

In *Cannery Row* Mary is always trying to keep Tom's spirits up when the rent is overdue and the electricity is about to be turned off and there is no money in sight. Mary's gaiety is infectious and usually keeps her husband from getting despondent. "We're going under," Talbot says. "No, we're not," she replies. "We're magic people. We always have been. Remember that ten dollars you found in a book—remember when your cousin sent you five dollars? Nothing can happen to us."

Talbot was, of course, Steinbeck, and Mary was Steinbeck's first wife, Carol. They were married in Los Angeles in 1930. Steinbeck described their "shack" at 2741 El Roble Drive in Eagle Rock as a "cheap place to live." They paid fifteen dollars per month for the place, which had, among other things, a thirty-foot living room with a giant stone fireplace, and a sleeping porch. Steinbeck enjoyed having people come and visit him, and he wrote to his friends from out of town suggesting that they come and "sit in front of a fire and talk, or lie on the beach and talk, or walk in the hills and talk." Later he would write in a letter to a friend: "Remember the days when we were living in Eagle Rock? As starved and happy a group as ever robbed an orange tree. I can still remember the dinners of hamburgers and stolen avocados."

According to Mike Spencer, who worked as a publicist for the Lung Association, Steinbeck was doing clerical work at the Association to keep alive. He was broke and not yet famous, still working on his second book, *To a God Unknown,* which didn't do well when it was finally published.

Steinbeck's stay in L.A. began in January of 1930 when there was lots of rain and cold, which made the fireplace an object of worship. But by August, not only was the light company about to turn off the juice, but Steinbeck was also complaining that it was "pretty hot down here now and my mind seems more sluggish than it usually is." The crowning blow came when the landlord, admiring all the fixing-up the Steinbecks had done on the house, evicted them so he could give it as a wedding present to his daughter. At this point, all the Steinbecks could think to do was get in their car and drive as far as their gas would get them. They ended up going back to Salinas, where Steinbeck's father and mother lived. His father gave the couple a small living allowance and a house in nearby Pacific Grove.

Three years later, Steinbeck had apparently forgotten the August and September heat of the Southland. He and Carol moved back to another outlying L.A. community—this time they lived at 2527 Hermosa Avenue in Montrose. By then Steinbeck was working on the final drafts of *To a God Unknown.* Again the time came when the rent was due and the utilities were about to be turned off. At this point, however, Steinbeck's mother became very ill, so the couple went up north for the final time. Steinbeck would later write magnificently of the poverty of the Dust Bowl Okies in *Grapes of Wrath,* but his own bottom-of-the-Depression stories occurred in Los Angeles.

Hollywood—the movie industry, that is, not the town—played only a minor part in drawing Henry Miller to Los Angeles. Miller, of course, spent the first and most productive part of his writing career as an expatriate from Brooklyn living in Paris during the Depression. On the eve of World War II he came back to his own country and his place in it, a process described in his book *The Air-Conditioned Nightmare,* which was about an automobile trip across the country. The book expressed Miller's rather dismal view of American culture, but it also indicated his belief that California was the only place where he saw any hope.

Critics do not now regard *The Air-Conditioned Nightmare* as one of Miller's great books, but in Los Angeles of the 1950s and '60s it was one of the treasured books of the young disenchanted intellectuals. Miller's philosophy was a curious combination of apolitical anarchism and resolute devotion to joy and happiness. His zest for life was expressed in his style, no matter how negative his intellectual perceptions of things.

Miller arrived in Hollywood in 1941 and began his early drafts of the book during his stay at the Gilbert Hotel, a seedy fleabag that is still there. He wasn't happy during his Hollywood stay, and he ended up going back to New York to finish the manuscript. But it wasn't long before he left New York forever to return to California. Here he discovered Steinbeck's biologist friend in Northern California, Ed Ricketts. In Southern California he had such friends as the famous British author Aldous Huxley and the not-so-famous artists Margaret and Gilbert Nieman, who lived in a rundown place on Bunker Hill. Miller liked visiting the Niemans, from whose porch he swore downtown L.A. looked like Paris—at least at night. Miller also used to hang out with the artist Man Ray in an apartment house across the street from the Hollywood Ranch Market on Vine Street.

When Miller returned to California for good, he lived for a while in L.A.'s Beverly Glen Canyon. Then he moved up to Big Sur, where he lived for some years. In the early '60s he returned to the Southland, purchased a house in Pacific Palisades, and spent the last two decades of his life there, writing books that were mostly published by Capra Press, a small press in Santa Barbara.

Although Miller lived in L.A. a long time, it must be admitted that much of his important work was done in the first part of his life. *The Air-Conditioned Nightmare* represented a bridge, and in the chronicle of his drive westward we are getting more than a simple travelogue.

The most interesting person he met in those travels was an old desert rat from the Barstow area. The desert rat talked a lot about automobiles, which he said were not only senseless killers, but had changed the country—in some ways for the better, but mostly for the worse. The desert rat talked about living in the desert with the stars and the rocks, "wondering about creation and that sort of thing." He uttered words that Miller obviously regarded as prophetic in 1941. "I figure," he said, "that when we get too close to the secret, nature has a way of getting rid of us." Miller anticipated a lot of '60s consciousness when he wrote about the Indians of the desert, whose life he contrasted favorably with the mundane, commercial, trivial, and brutal culture of white America.

In Barstow it was too hot to go on right away. Miller discovered, however, that he couldn't just linger in a restaurant without ordering food or beverage, which had been his habit in Paris. So, realizing that it was Mother's Day, he went to the railway station to send his mother a telegram. That completed, he sat under a tree at the railway station and suddenly fell into a reverie, for this was the same old railway station that he had seen in 1913 when he made his brief visit to the Southland. That was the time he ended up in Chula Vista, "burning brush all day in a broiling sun," and in San Diego hearing a speech by Emma Goldman. It was a speech that changed his life, he said. He also spent time during his 1913 visit looking for a job as a cowboy on a cattle ranch in the San Pedro area.

By the time he got to Burbank, these memories of Southern California not long after the turn of the century had been doused. "I tried to summon a feeling of devotion in memory of Luther Burbank, but the traffic was too thick, and there was no parking space. Perhaps they had named it after another Burbank, the king of soda water or popcorn or laminated valves." (Actually, Burbank was named after a dentist who was one of the city's founding fathers.)

The first night in Hollywood, Miller ended up at a millionaire's party. He didn't like the assortment of businessmen, aged strike-breakers, football players, and flag wavers he met there. One drunken, garrulous lout especially annoyed him. The lout asked Miller how he liked California. So Miller went on and on explaining that this wasn't his first visit to the Golden State. He said that he'd been here once before, doing a stretch at San Quentin for attempted murder. He explained that he hadn't known the revolver was loaded when he took a potshot at his sister and luckily missed her. He complained that the judge hadn't understood the circumstances of the shooting and had sentenced him to prison. As Miller's story got more and more bizarre, the lout got more and more uncomfortable, and finally disappeared. Not much later, Miller was walking north on Cahuenga Boulevard toward the hills, "looking up at the stars when a car came up behind me and ran into a lamppost. Everyone was killed. I walked on 'irregardless,' as they say."

Interesting to ponder is the encounter between L.A. and Jack Kerouac, who was the very soul of the restless wanderer in the 1950s. Kerouac was known as the King of the Beats, although it was not a title he had sought out and, in fact, he tried to reject it. Restlessness was a hallmark of such California writers as Jack London, Mark Twain, and Robinson Jeffers. But usually they came to terms with their wanderlust and found a piece of the planet with which to identify at the end. Kerouac never did. He was the eternal wanderer.

The most clear-cut influence on Kerouac was California's own Jack London, who wrote a book of hoboing experiences called *The Road*. The book that made Kerouac famous was *On the Road*, published in 1951. In *Lonesome Traveler*, which appeared in 1961, Kerouac was still writing about wandering. Oddly enough, *Lonesome Traveler* begins with a description of Kerouac coming into Los Angeles on a freight train in 1951, and *On the Road* begins with Kerouac riding a freight train away from Los Angeles. In both cases he was riding the "Zipper"—the fast Southern Pacific night freight—but one was southbound and the other northbound. Although he was cold, riding as a hobo in an open car, Kerouac felt a tremendous sense of aliveness and even health as the Zipper flew past Santa Barbara, past Surf, and onward to Guadalupe and Oceano in *On the Road*. In *Lonesome Traveler*, Kerouac was riding in the Zipper's heated caboose, legally, because he had worked as a brakeman in the Southern Pacific's Texas division; but he was suffering from a virus. As he headed toward L.A. he was so miserable that he was unable to "appreciate a good ride" as the train "flashed past the snowy breaking surf caps at Surf and Tangair and Gaviota on the division that runs the moony rail between San Luis Obispo and Santa Barbara."

When Kerouac arrived in downtown Los Angeles in *Lonesome Traveler*, he checked himself into a hotel on Main Street and treated himself nicely by taking "bourbon lemon juice and Anacin" for twenty-four hours and looking out the window at the "hot sunny streets of L.A. Christmas." After a while he bestirred himself and checked out the pool halls and shoeshine places on Skid Row, just to kill time. He was due to go down to the L.A. harbor at San Pedro, to meet his friend Deni, who was due in on the S.S. *Roamer*. (It is probably not coincidence that London owned a boat called *The Roamer*.) Deni had promised Kerouac he could get him a job on the S.S. *Roamer*, and on the strength of that, Kerouac had come across the country to Los Angeles for this evening.

It was Christmas night, 1951, in San Pedro. The *Roamer* came in and Deni got off. Deni first wanted to go up to Hollywood and see the stars and have some fun. "After a fast hike of about twenty minutes along those dreary refineries and waterskeel slaphouse stop holes, under impossible skies laden I suppose with stars but you could just see their dirty blur in the Southern California Christmas," Kerouac and Deni arrived at the Red Car tracks, where they would be whisked up to Hollywood.

First, however, Deni wanted to go into the hotel in downtown San Pedro across from the Red Car stop. "Someone was supposed to meet us with the blondes," Deni told Kerouac. "The hotel had potted palms and potted barfronts and cars parked, and everything dead and windless with the dead California sad windless smokesmog," Kerouac noted. Kerouac's further descriptions of the hotel indicated that the vacuous young men and women of today's glitter·generation were with us even then. So were the "hotrod champion sons of aircraft computators of Long Beach, the whole general and really dismal California culture."

They decided to look for a quick beer. Deni warned Kerouac to avoid places with lots of Mexicans: "They're *pachucos,* they just like to beat up on people for the hell of it." Kerouac replied that when he was in Mexico it didn't seem to him that the Mexicans were that way. Deni agreed that Mexicans were different in Mexico, but somehow turned it around so he was accusing Kerouac of being the kind of person who worried about the starving multitudes of Europe.

Then Deni realized they had better catch the last Red Car if they were going to see the "glitters of Los Angeles if possible or Hollywood before all the bars closed." The last train, however, had just pulled out. Deni insisted on hiring a taxi to catch up with it, but the taxi driver wasn't fast enough. The Red Car clipped along at over sixty miles per hour "towards Compton and environs of L.A." and also seemed to tow the reader on into the next chapter and yet another installment of the Kerouac cosmos.

Deni—predictably enough—had no job for Kerouac aboard the *Roamer.* And no money to lend Kerouac. As the *Roamer* pulled out of San Pedro harbor, Kerouac watched it go and didn't seem terribly sad at its departure without him. For suddenly he had a strong vision of the *Roamer* as a floating metal prison. He shrugged and headed down Mexico way.

Kerouac's view of L.A. was obviously that of someone just passing through. But there is something of the "just passing through" quality in Steinbeck's and even Miller's encounters with the place. Perhaps there was a kind of synergistic relationship between L.A. and writers; the combination of restless authors and an ever-changing, transitory town helped produce a new vision in American literature. For Kerouac, there was nothing in L.A. that reached out and asked him to stay, as there had been for Miller and maybe almost for Steinbeck. Still, the fact that Kerouac opened both of his books with L.A. suggests something of the city's lodestone qualities for a writer. L.A. was a sort of literary, if disillusioning, Eldorado.

TWO

Down and Out
at the Brown Derby with
Malcolm Lowry

Malcolm Lowry
Late of the Bowery
His prose was flowery
And often glowery
He lived, nightly, and drank daily
And died playing the ukelele.

[Malcolm Lowry's self-composed epitaph]

The recent eruptions of Mount St. Helens reminded me of a terrifying, powerful book called Under the Volcano. Malcolm Lowry's masterpiece is a nightmarish, hallucinogenic vision of a man's descent into purgatory. The book's main character is a self-destructive drunk in Cuernavaca, Mexico, who is flung into the abyss, literally under the volcano Popocatepetl.

Lowry's protagonist—a figure who is almost entirely autobiographical—is called simply "the Consul." The Consul had been serving as a British diplomat in

Cuernavaca, but by the Day of the Dead in 1939, England had broken off relations with Mexico. The inevitability of the coming World War pervades the book, and the story is not only of one man drinking himself to death: it is about a whole world plunging into the abyss.

Malcolm Lowry lived in Los Angeles during that fateful year of 1939. And while most of the book was written in Vancouver, Canada, and the action takes place in Mexico, there is a strong Los Angeles connection in *Under the Volcano.*

When Lowry died in his native England in 1957 at forty-eight years of age, little of his work had been published since *Under the Volcano* in 1947. *Dark As the Grave Wherein My Friend is Laid* was not published until the late '60s, along with several of his uncompleted works. *Dark As the Grave* is a thinly fictionalized version of a trip Lowry took from Canada back to Mexico in the last days of the Second World War. Lowry's alter ego in *Dark As the Grave* is taking his wife Priscilla back to Cuernavaca. (Priscilla's real-life model was Margerie Bonner, Lowry's second wife, whom he met in 1938 during his longest stay in Los Angeles, where he landed after being ejected by the Mexican authorities on his first visit.)

During a longish stopover at the Los Angeles airport in *Dark As the Grave* we find the Lowry alter ego thinking about Los Angeles, and his thoughts are not flattering. He thinks of the "barren deathscape of Los Angeles, and yet it was in this hell they met." He's impressed by how Los Angeles has changed through the war years, while he has been away in Canada with Priscilla. Other cities had big new airports, but "it was that the mode of travel on this great new scale was new itself, and no airport could have absolutely expressed this newness better than Los Angeles, than this huge gray-sounding place with its tremendous sense of junction, to north, south, east and west."

At another point in his musings, the Lowry figure admits to having hated Los Angeles "so violently"

that on occasion "all he could think was that it was a hell, the sort of hell his spirit would have wandered to had he killed himself." To Lowry, L.A. was a junction between heaven and hell—although more hell than heaven.

Lowry was at his greatest, of course, in writing about hell, since his life was lived in one. To UCLA English professor Richard K. Cross, whose *Malcolm Lowry: A Preface to His Fiction* has been published recently by the University of Chicago Press, "Lowry saw Los Angeles as the dissolving edge of civilization. He did not like Los Angeles."

Cross says that Lowry, whose reputation has been growing since his death, wrote one of the eight or perhaps ten best novels of the century in *Under the Volcano.* Cross says that Lowry's book puts him on a level with such twentieth-century masters as Thomas Mann, James Joyce, Joseph Conrad, and Franz Kafka. "Lowry was an important writer," Cross told me, "who just couldn't do it again."

Lowry was born in Cheshire, England, in 1909. His father was a prosperous international trader, but Lowry felt more identity with his Norwegian sea-captain grandfather on his mother's side. The books of Jack London inspired Lowry to join the merchant marine as a young man. He was driven to his ship's side in a Rolls Royce limousine, which of course made it difficult for him to be accepted by the other seamen. Lowry recorded those adventures in his first novel, *Ultramarine,* which was published in London in 1933. The book had an indifferent success. The rest of his life, Lowry labored in obscurity, except for the brief flurry of attention that came his way because of *Under the Volcano,* the only other book of his to be published in his lifetime.

He gained a reputation as a genius and a drunk early on, especially among his peers at Cambridge. Nearly everyone who came into contact with this short, barrel-chested man—a man who couldn't find his way in a city, who was given to constant mishaps and misadventures—sensed that they were in the presence of genius.

Lowry met his first wife Jan Gabrial in Paris in 1933, in the home of his mentor, the writer Conrad Aiken. Like the second wife he was to find later in Los Angeles, the first was an American. But Gabrial was not at all like the faithful and adoring Margerie, who helped her helpless husband function. Rather, Gabrial complained about the poverty of their life, and wondered why they were poor if everyone was convinced that Lowry was such a genius. It was a stormy marriage from the beginning. Lowry kept drinking, and Gabrial left for days and even weeks on trips with other lovers, which only drove Lowry to more drinking. Jan obviously became the "bad" part of Yvonne, the Consul's former wife in *Under the Volcano,* who comes back to Mexico to save her husband but also makes love with Hugh, the Consul's communist half-brother, and M. Laruelle, a friend of the Consul and a washed-up film-maker.

Much of what is known about Jan Gabrial came from Aiken, who said she had a "strong social conscience" but was, on the whole, a rotten woman. Aiken, however, was hardly an objective third party—he too had been her lover, and in *Ushant* portrayed her as the lover of both men. It fell to an old Cambridge buddy of Lowry's, the critic John Davenport, to tell Lowry that Gabrial was involved with a lot of old writer friends. (Davenport, incidentally, was the one who went to Los Angeles and convinced Lowry he ought to go there too. But that was later.) "Malc simply couldn't cope with a woman like Jan," Davenport said. "His deep sense of sexual inadequacy—a characteristic of the Consul too—probably stems from the situation with Jan."

Finally she left Lowry in Paris and went back to her native New York. But Lowry, who seemed really to love her, soon followed. Perhaps Lowry would inevitably have come to the New World, in any event. His biggest loves, after drink, were jazz (he played the ukelele, as his epitaph noted, and had even published some songs in London) and Herman Melville.

Had other things been equal, Melville alone might have attracted him to the New World. Melville and Lowry not only labored in obscurity to produce one great masterpiece, but both attached great symbolic importance to things: in Lowry's case it was a volcano, in Melville's a whale.

Lowry successfully reunited with Gabrial in New York, but he also was treated in Bellevue for his worsening alcoholism. After Bellevue, they decided to make a new start elsewhere—so they took a bus to Los Angeles.

At the same time Lowry's old friend Davenport was going to Los Angeles by train to take a studio writing assignment. Davenport left telegrams scattered across the country at strategic bus stops, telling Malcolm and Jan they could stay with him when they got to Los Angeles—which they did, for a couple of months.

Lowry's ending up in Los Angeles was not as unexpected as it might have seemed. *Under the Volcano* has been called the most cinematic novel ever written. Lowry was fascinated by films, and badly wanted to work in Hollywood, according to Davenport. But there was no work in 1936. Years later Margerie would insist that Malcolm had indeed worked on a number of scripts during his first stay in Los Angeles, but was unhappy with the mediocrity that was expected, and abhorred team-writing. Davenport said that the only work he knew of Lowry doing was work he himself gave to Lowry. So perhaps it was economics that drove Malcolm and Jan to leave San Pedro and arrive in Acapulco on the Day of the Dead in 1936. Living was cheaper in Mexico than in Los Angeles, which meant that father Arthur O. Lowry's dole would go a little further there.

Whatever the circumstances of Lowry's first departure from Los Angeles, his going to Mexico proved to be fateful for him. "Like Columbus I have torn through one reality and discovered another," Lowry wrote in a letter to a friend toward the end of his infamous two-year stay in Cuernavaca, under Popocatepetl and its twin volcano far to the east, Ixtacihuatl. As Professor Cross says in his book on Lowry, "It was by no means the last of Lowry's perilous voyages, but it was undoubtedly the most decisive, as crucial for him as the journey up the Congo had been for Conrad."

Malcolm and Jan were undoubtedly attracted to Cuernavaca partly because there were lots of foreigners there already, and many were literary types. But another attraction had to be the abundance of tequila and mescal. A Lowry biographer described Cuernavaca as both a "drunkard's paradise and hell." After two years there, Jan was gone, and Lowry himself was not-so-gently escorted from the country — although it's not clear if he was officially deported, since he made a second trip back after the war, with equally disastrous results.

Although Lowry saw Mexico as an "age-old arena of racial and political conflicts," and even mentioned how the great California writer Ambrose Bierce found his death there, the Mexico Lowry wrote about was as much his own "inner landscape" as an objective reality. Alcohol undoubtedly added to his paranoid visions. Still, the reality of Mexico then was that it had a leftist president named Cardenas who had kicked out the foreign oil corporations and was trying to help the poor, while at the same time the military and police were being infiltrated by Nazi agents from Germany who sought a means of threatening the United States.

Plainly Lowry was finding echoes of the Spanish Civil War in Mexican politics of the time as well. Lowry had lost some of his friends from Cambridge, who had fought with the Loyalists in Spain against Franco. It is not just coincidence that at the end of the Day of the Dead in *Under the Volcano*, the Consul is killed by the local military police because they think he is a Jew, a communist, and a spy. He is, of course, none of these things.

It was obvious later to various of his friends who saw Lowry in Mexico that he was living the life of his Consul. Jan disappeared with her lovers for days on end, and finally she just packed up and went back to Los Angeles. Meanwhile Lowry was drinking — once he drank for twenty-four hours a day for three days and two nights without sleeping. Yet somehow he also got a start on the manuscript of *Under the Volcano*, and had a forty-thousand-word manuscript completed before he returned to Los Angeles in July, 1938. In his alcoholic perambulations, however, the first draft was lost before he got back to L.A. (Lowry would lose more than one manuscript in his life through various and sundry mishaps — indeed he would eventually lose his life through mishap. The original draft of his first novel, *Ultramarine*, had been lost by an editor, so he had to recreate it in a hurry, and was never happy with the result. In fact, Lowry barely recovered one of the last drafts of *Under the Volcano*, which was finally published in 1947, from a fire which destroyed his home.)

Aiken was one of those who saw Lowry in Mexico, and he noted Jan's cold indifference to Lowry's plight in *Ushant*. Lowry, said Aiken, was becoming less and less the lighthearted mystic and more and more a fanatic one. He was obsessed with cabalistic structure, and his novel is clearly built around the cabalistic tree of life. He kept his trousers up with a necktie knotted around his waist; his face was becoming red and rounder. Toward the end of his stay in Mexico, Lowry was forever being thrown into dingy jails in the interior in order to dry out, only to be released to drag himself to the closest cantina to order his beloved, hallucinogenic mescal.

Finally the Mexican authorities decided to get him out of the country. At one point, as he was being held in prison before his deportation, he was asked by prison authorities who he was, and the answer he got became a famous line in *Under the Volcano*. "You say you are a wrider," Lowry quoted the authorities as saying to him, "but we read all your wridings and dey don't make sense. You no wrider, you an espider, and we shoota de espiders in Mexico." Lowry said he took the word espider to mean spy.

Toward the end of his stay Lowry wrote his father, trying to make the worse appear the better. "We had a good deal of bother lately," he wrote in a cheerfully vague manner, "what with our house being robbed and leaving Mexico . . . so we decided each to get jobs, Jan going to Los Angeles for a bit, I on assignment here of an innocent nature." His "assignment" was his drinking himself to death, of course.

Arthur Lowry's lawyers took charge. Malcolm was put on a train in Mexico City by his father's agents and changed trains at Nogales, Arizona, for Los Angeles. He was met on his arrival in L.A. by his father's attorney here, Benjamin Parks, and immediately taken to the Hotel Normandie, now a retirement home on Normandie near Wilshire Boulevard. He was declared an incompetent by the State of California. Parks paid his hotel bill and gave him a tiny bit of money for food and cigarettes.

At the same time, Jan accepted a "sizeable cash settlement" in lieu of divorce alimony, according to Douglas Day in his biography *Malcolm Lowry*. She took the money and ran, with a lover, to Santa Barbara. But she turned up in Lowry's life a few more times before disappearing from view forever. Once she wrote a letter to Lowry, after he had moved to Canada with Margerie, saying she'd like to get together for old times' sake. Lowry tore up her letter and never answered it. She also wrote a thinly-veiled fictional account of what had happened in Mexico; it was published and apparently hit home with Lowry, who was depressed by it.

But that was all later. For the moment, Lowry had settled down to writing at the Hotel Normandie— writing poems about Mexico, and possibly working on a new draft of *Under the Volcano*. A woman down the hall was said to be typing the new version. It has long been a mystery just when and where Lowry began this second draft, which is really the first extant draft of *Under the Volcano* and was finished in Canada in 1941. "No one really knows," says Professor Cross, "where it was begun. It's anybody's guess."

What is known for sure is that he was lonely most of the year he spent in Los Angeles. His old English friends Davenport and Arthur Calder-Marshall had left Hollywood. He wrote long letters to people around the world. To Nordahl Grieg, the Norwegian novelist who was almost as much a mentor as Aiken, he wrote from the Hotel Normandie: "I have been married, lost my wife, and been importuned by fascists. I had a terrible sojourn in Mexico. I am but a skeleton—thank God—of my former self." To Aiken he wrote that Jan had left him a sort of Lear of the Sierras, dying by the glass in the Brown Derby, in Hollywood. "I don't blame her, I was better off in the Brown Derby."

One of his only friends during that period was another tenant of the Hotel Normandie, one Jack King. It was King who changed Lowry's life by introducing him to Margerie Bonner, of whom Lowry would later say that he "had unlocked her from the prison of Los Angeles."

Margerie Bonner was a true child of Hollywood— her mother brought her and her sister Priscilla to Tinseltown from Michigan. Priscilla was just starting to play starring film roles (opposite comedian Harry Langdon, for example) when her eyes were blinded by klieg lights, cutting short her career. Margerie then began to find some success in playing young-horsewoman roles in westerns, and when she was not working as an actress, she was churning out scripts either for radio or for Disney cartoons. She also had some of her detective novels published. So she was indeed a professional writer.

There's long been a raging debate, however, over how much of *Under the Volcano* she wrote. She certainly rewrote and edited Lowry's later works, which were issued after his death. At one point in Canada

Malcolm wrote Priscilla a letter describing how "we" are working on a book—the book he was referring to was *Under the Volcano.*

Today both Margerie and Priscilla live in Beverly Hills. Margerie Lowry is seventy-five and recently had a severe stroke, which left her unable to talk. Priscilla says, with regard to her sister's feelings for Lowry, "I think she blocked out the horrors and kept the good parts. There's been a great deal said about his drunkenness, but there were long periods, especially when they lived in Vancouver, when he was industrious and sober. Those were the happiest years of her life."

Priscilla said that Lowry's friend at the hotel, Jack King, a salesman for a pharmaceutical house, had known Lowry from China during the latter's sailing days. One day he called Margerie, who was a friend, and announced that he could recommend this gentleman most highly, he was an Englishman and so forth, would she have dinner with him?

According to King, as reported in the biography *Malcolm Lowry,* it was a case of love at first sight. Malcolm called Margerie on the phone first, and they agreed to meet at the corner of Western and Hollywood. Lowry took a bus to the meeting. King was a few seconds late. By the time he arrived, they were embracing—and still embracing several moments later.

Two weeks later, in what was surely not a coincidence, Lowry was ushered from the Hotel Normandie by attorney Parks, no doubt on Arthur Lowry's insistence. Parks told Lowry he had to get ready to leave Los Angeles right away, that he had to go to Canada to renew his visa. He wouldn't even allow Lowry to go down the hall to the typist who was working on *Under the Volcano,* although he promised that he would fetch it and mail it to Lowry, which he did. Lowry's biographer, Day, says that Lowry really didn't have to go to Canada—most likely the senior Lowry was unhappy at the money he had to settle on

Jan Gabrial, and wasn't anxious to have his son become involved again.

Margerie was in Lowry's room when Parks arrived. As Lowry was driven away from the hotel, he hung out the rear window of Parks's car, yelling to her that he would be back. And he did try.

After a few days in Vancouver, Canada, Lowry boarded a bus headed back to Los Angeles. A poem about that experience—admittedly not a good one, Lowry said—can be found in *Dark As the Grave.*

A singing smell of tar, of the highway,
Fills the gray Vancouver Bus Terminal
Crowned by dreaming names, Portland,
  New Orleans,
Spokane, Chicago—and Los Angeles!
City of the angels and my luck—

The trip back to Los Angeles was another typical Lowry misadventure. He got drunk, and when he got to Blaine, Washington, the immigration authorities turned him back. After that, Lowry started to go into a rapid decline. But Margerie quit her job as a secretary to Penny Singleton, Hollywood's "Blondie," and was with him within a month of his leaving the Hotel Normandie.

Lowry was not an easy person to live with—he had frequent rages, black moods, childish tantrums, and later, when he went back to serious boozing, he became violent and threatening. Because of his experience with Jan Gabrial, he would never fully trust even Margerie.

At first Lowry hated Canada; he wanted to take Margerie back to Los Angeles. "Margerie is American, helpless and utterly without money," he complained in a letter to Aiken, "and were she deported to Hollywood she would have nothing to live on, and moreover she would be, for many reasons, in an untenable position and also could not stand being without me." But they persevered in Vancouver—they found an uninsulated, poorly heated squatter's shack in the country outside of Vancouver. The nearest bar was ten miles away.

By 1941, the "second draft" of *Under the Volcano* was completed and was, in turn, rejected by a host of publishers. Lowry went back to improving it, and by 1946 he found both an English and an American publisher. Critics compared Lowry to James Joyce and Thomas Wolfe when the book was published the following year. He even made the cover of the *Saturday Review.* He responded to the adulation by drinking more.

The book sold thirty thousand copies, which was good but not stupendous. The last ten years of his life became more and more difficult – at one point Margerie had a nervous breakdown. Still, she stuck by him, even after a doctor warned her that if she didn't leave him he would kill her, much as the Consul kills Yvonne in *Under the Volcano.*

During his last days in England, Lowry dreamed of going back to Canada, which had begun to claim him as its greatest writer. There had been good times in Canada for both the Lowrys. Once in Vancouver, for instance, there was a telling meeting between Lowry and his old friend, the great Welsh poet Dylan Thomas. "How is ruddy old Malc?" Thomas had asked before the meeting. Then when they met it was a simple warm clasping of hands. "Hullo Dylan," Malcolm said, and Thomas replied in the same shy way. Not much later, of course, Thomas would die from his alcoholism, just as Lowry would. The poet and the novelist were men who lived under that same volcano, but nonetheless were possessed of an incredible creative ferment. Perhaps it was the combination of the transcendent qualities of mystical inebriation and their natively outsized talents that produced the great works of each.

Both were hopeless drunks – in Lowry's case not even the love of Margerie could save him. He went through apomorphine aversion treatment in London before the doctors simply gave up on him. He was locked in a tiny cell illuminated by only a red bulb, given injections of apomorphine, and allowed all the alcohol he wanted to drink. The combination produces nausea and vomiting, and supposedly builds a conditioned response against ever drinking again. Most patients can't survive five days of this torture, but Lowry was going strong after twenty days. And within forty-eight hours of his release, he was back drinking in a pub.

After his death in 1957, Margerie worked to complete his manuscripts, although much of the paradise part of Lowry's intended *Divine Comedy* was lost in a fire that destroyed their Canadian shack – the same fire that almost consumed *Under the Volcano.* She never remarried. "She would have never remarried," her sister told me, "for she was married to Malcolm for eternity, at least as far as she was concerned."

Just how much of *Under the Volcano* belonged to Los Angeles? If you were counting even only Margerie, the answer would be quite a bit. But another big ingredient was Hollywood, for despite his disdain for Tinseltown, *Under the Volcano* was more influenced by cinema than any single novel. In Vancouver, the Lowrys had worked on a movie script of Fitzgerald's *Tender is the Night,* with the hope that it might be used by MGM. It wasn't used, but it is said to be a brilliant script.

A more direct line to Los Angeles was the influence on *Under the Volcano* of Russian filmmaker Sergei Eisenstein's *Thunder Over Mexico.* That film was the result of Charlie Chaplin's introduction of Eisenstein, who was then looking for work in Hollywood, to Upton Sinclair, who agreed to produce the movie. *Under the Volcano* obviously owes a great debt to *Thunder Over Mexico,* particularly the powerful imagery of the Day of the Dead.

There are scenes toward the end of *Under the Volcano* in which Yvonne remembers her early days as a starlet in Hollywood. She attempts a comeback after being a child star. "She received promises, and that was all. In the end she walked down Virgil Avenue or Mariposa beneath the dusty dead shallow-plant palms of the dark and accursed City of the Angels without even the consolation that her tragedy was no less valid for being so stale."

No, Lowry knew something about Los Angeles in the late '30s, something that may not have been all pretty, something that may have been his own private hell as much as it was the real city, but still something real. Although Lowry hated Los Angeles, it was inevitable that he come to Los Angeles, as inevitable as was everything in the Consul's life. Death was the bottom of the cabalistic down-cycle that had to come before life. The plunge into the darkness taken by both the Consul and the world in 1939 is best summed up in the last words of *Under the Volcano*. They are: "Somebody threw a dead dog after him down the ravine."

THREE

The Day of the Locust:
The Greatest Hollywood
Novel of Them All

O n a hot summer day, if you walk up the steep incline on Ivar Street just north of Yucca, it might seem as if nothing much has changed since Nathanael West sat in a dingy room in the Parva-Sed Apta apartment hotel in 1935 and began writing the greatest Hollywood novel of them all—The Day of the Locust.

The automobiles look different, of course, and a couple of places that are on the hill now obviously weren't there during the middle of the

Depression. But the Parva-Sed Apta, which translates from the Latin as "small but suitable," probably doesn't look so different now than it did then—at least from the outside. A cross between Tudor and Black Forest cottage, it has an important-looking though shabby facade. "Parva-Sed Apta" is emblazoned on the door glass, complete with the hyphen, which was a common affectation of the twenties.

The Parva-Sed Apta was the oldest building on the hill, even older than the Alto Nido, which sprawls on the hilltop above it. There's still a remnant of all the stained glass that was in the building when West lived there. The glass is believed to have come from an old church when the building was built in 1923.

Once you get past the lobby, the building looks like any other shabby Hollywood rooming house. West put it this way in *The Day of the Locust:* "Another name for Ivar Street was Lysol Alley." And in case that doesn't make the point, he explains: "The rent was high because it included police protection, a service for which he [West's protagonist] had no need."

West used the inhabitants of the Parva-Sed Apta as models for many of the characters in *The Day of the Locust,* although his physical description of the fictional San Bernardino Arms is modeled on another nearby building. The movie version of *The Day of the Locust* used one of the fancy buildings over on Rossmore.

Today you will find many of the same kinds of people living at the Parva-Sed Apta as were there in the mid-thirties. James Udall Sr., the Westwood realtor who was the building's leasing agent when West lived there, says he remembers most of the inhabitants as "clerks" and so forth. But how many self-proclaimed writers and actors and musicians admit these kinds of aspirations to landlords? The building's owner, Dr. Frank Pierce, who has had it in his family since the early thirties, suggests that it certainly has had its ups and downs, as witness the fact that he had to remove much of the stained glass to his own house in Beverly Hills in order to save it from tenants intent on tearing the place apart. But the Parva-Sed's current manager is a bright-enough-seeming gent named Michael Leo Michaud, who hands you a business card that announces that he's not a property manager but an assistant cameraman. To listen to him, things at the Parva-Sed haven't changed all that much from the way West said it was, back in the old days.

While Michaud is dealing with what looks like either an eviction or a landlord-tenant controversy of some dire sort, and at the same time keeping tabs on a young woman who looks like she's done a bit of heroin in her time and whom he obviously doesn't want around his building, he explains that most of the inhabitants are "filmmakers." You assume by looking around at the place that they have not yet become successful filmmakers, but suddenly a fellow on the front porch starts talking rather intelligently and knowledgeably about Upton Sinclair and Sergei Eisenstein.

West, no doubt, would have understood Michaud—West was a hotel manager and night clerk himself, in New York, before he got his first job in a Hollywood studio. He came to Hollywood in 1933 for a job writing scripts, on the strength of his sale of *Miss Lonelyhearts* to Twentieth Century-Fox for four thousand dollars, even though the novel itself had sold poorly. He stayed only a few months.

It was when West returned to Hollywood from the East Coast in 1935 that he moved into the Parva-Sed Apta. He said he did it in part because he wanted to live in a genuine Hollywood rooming house so he could research his next book. In *The Day of the Locust,* West was not writing about the movers and the shakers of Hollywood, as his good friend F. Scott Fitzgerald was in *The Last Tycoon.* West was writing about the lower depths, the sea of hopefuls from which the chosen few emerge. Unlike so many writers who came to Hollywood, West was rather good at separating his life's work, writing novels, from his hack work, which was grinding out scenarios, mostly for "B" movies.

Hundreds of novels have been published about Hollywood; one estimate is that there have been at least fifteen hundred titles. Naturally, only a few of these have been very good. Certainly one must include Evelyn Waugh's *The Loved One,* Raymond Chandler's works, *The Last Tycoon,* and perhaps even Budd Schulberg's *What Makes Sammy Run?* But many critics contend that the elusive essence of Hollywood was best captured in West's novel.

To many who are familiar with that vague section of the Los Angeles area called Hollywood, *The Day of the Locust* captures its apocalyptic mood, a mood that doesn't seem to have lessened that much in the last half-century. It isn't just that one is reminded at every corner that the creation of fantasy on celluloid is the primary enterprise here; it is also the fact that so many of the apartment buildings are unreinforced masonry doomed to extinction when the inevitable big earthquake strikes. The orgy/riot climax of West's novel seems metaphorically to pinpoint this madness.

To some, however, it is a book about a Hollywood that no longer exists. One view of how Hollywood has changed comes from Ken Hense, a real estate appraiser and a keen observer of the Hollywood cultural scene. After seeing the movie and rereading the book, he offered the view that back in West's time "there was still a lot of hope as well as innocence" about Hollywood. He suggests that this is no longer as true, that the Hollywood population has gained a substratum that has no aspirations to glamour. The glamour is gone.

Not so for West in that summer of 1935, when he became involved in the lives of the Parva-Sed's tenants, characters he described not as "clerks," but as aspiring actors and actresses, seedy comics, prostitutes, broken-down vaudeville performers, stunt men, technicians, and a particularly repulsive dwarf.

Understand that although there was a Depression on, Hollywood was a boom town when West first arrived, almost in the manner of San Francisco during the Gold Rush. The early thirties were especially good for writers, because talkies were still coming in, and there was a big need for scripts. Films were becoming a major industry in the country during the Depression—one of the nation's top ten industries, in fact. And it was an industry centered in Los Angeles.

West had come from an affluent family that was wiped out financially by the Depression. West's sister Laura, however, had married his old college chum, S.J. Perelman. Perelman became not only West's lifelong admirer but also his patron. During West's Parva-Sed days it was only as a result of Perelman's generosity that West was able to survive even in a modest manner. Even if he had been able to get work, it is doubtful he would have been able to do it. He was ill during part of his stay at the Parva-Sed.

For days on end, West didn't leave his room. He felt that he was building up a giant debt to his brother-in-law which he'd never be able to pay, that he was a failure as a writer who'd never get a job. It's understandable that West felt this way; his imagined problems were being compounded by real physical ones. Not only was he suffering from gonorrhea, no doubt obtained from another tenant in the Parva-Sed; he was also suffering from a flare-up of an old prostrate problem. He was in terrible pain, for which the doctor gave him morphine. He was losing weight, and looking more and more like a scarecrow. He couldn't sleep, and could hardly sit on a chair for more than ten minutes.

Some critics have professed to have great insights into *The Day of the Locust,* based on their interpretations of West's sexual nature. But in point of fact his circumstances were not conducive to a healthy appreciaion of sex during that period of his life. He was floating in a sea of characters who somehow seemed to sum up the human condition; they were like characters out of paintings of the damned. *The Day of the Locust* reads like a painting in many ways, and that's not accidental. West was something of an artist himself, and like his protagonist, Todd Hackett, he had been an art student. Moreover, the novel has his strong sense of the surreal, the absurd, the ironic and the perverse.

For example, West owned a car during the period he was at the Parva-Sed, and he often lent it to the prostitutes so it would be easier for them to conduct their business. This tickled West immensely.

It is, of course, no surprise that the language of the madam and prostitute, the aspiring actresses, the racetrack enthusiasts, and the out-and-out con artists, was so beautifully incorporated into the book.

In *The Day of the Locust,* the whole creating mechanism of Hollywood seemed to be lubricated by dope and sex and other assorted cheap thrills. One day someone asked West to store a suitcase. He did, until several weeks later he became suspicious, opened it, and found it full of marijuana. He disposed of the dope through his underworld connections.

His room at the Parva-Sed was "quite horrid," consisting mainly of a Murphy bed and a kitchenette. The summer heat was terrific, and sometimes as he lay in bed he felt as if the whole of Los Angeles were an inferno. Not only was it summertime, but the rim of the sky above the "ugly" but "almost beautiful" Hollywood Hills was filled with smoke. The air rang with the sound of fire trucks going up and down the canyon. At night, unable to eat or sleep, West watched the glow of the flames complete the picture.

Throughout the book Hackett is working on a painting called "The Burning of Los Angeles." West described Hackett's work this way: "He was going to show the city burning at high noon, so that the flames would have to compete with the desert sun. . . . He wanted the city to have quite a gala air as it burned."

West was not always on his back dreaming burning nightmares in bed at the Parva-Sed. When he was well, he loved to cruise Hollywood Boulevard, and was a perennial fixture in front of Musso & Frank's Grill, where he would stand chewing a toothpick, assessing the surroundings intently. He was an acclaimed cohort of the many celebrated writers who gathered there, and also next door at Stanley Rose's bookstore, now gone. These writers may have been in Hollywood only because of movie work, but when they gathered they did not talk movies, they talked literature. Among them were John O'Hara, Erskine Caldwell, William Saroyan, William Faulkner, F. Scott Fitzgerald, and Dashiell Hammett.

In 1936, even though he was working again and had left the Parva-Sed, West still sought sleaze. In his pursuit of the underworld, he became almost as much of a fixture in the pressrooms downtown. He got to know police-beat reporters and went out on calls with them. He was particularly intrigued by domestic murders, which usually were over money. He enjoyed Filipino dance halls, and he was an inveterate cockfight attender—one of the greatest scenes in *The Day of the Locust* is the cockfight scene in a garage in Beachwood Canyon. West may have actually attended such a cockfight, but generally he went to Wilmington or even as far away as Pismo Beach, two hundred miles up the coast from L.A.

Another Los Angeles phenomenon West found fascinating enough to describe in *The Day of the Locust* was Sister Aimee Semple McPherson's temple (officially called the Angelus Temple, which still overlooks Echo Park Lake; it probably is not mere coincidence that L.A., which has long been known to writers and readers as Lotus Land, houses the nation's biggest lotus collection in Echo Park, a gift from the mystic East, given by Sister McPherson in the twenties). West was also fascinated by Grauman's Chinese Theater and used to go there to watch premieres. The last scene in *The Day of the Locust* occurs at "Kahn's Pleasure Dome," which is, of course, a combination of the pleasure dome in Coleridge's "Kubla Khan" and Grauman's Chinese Theater.

All West ever made from his four books, during his lifetime, was a little more than eight hundred dollars. Yet "it's fair," his biographer, Jay Martin, insists, "to put him in the category of Hemingway and Fitzgerald — perhaps he wasn't as great a writer as Tolstoy or Faulkner or Malcolm Lowry. His was a very condensed kind of writing, directly connected to human psychology, rather than a representation of society, manners or morals."

In a very basic sense, West was out of step with his age, which might account for the fact that his books didn't sell well until after his death. Like so many during the Depression, West was a communist sympathizer and even a political activist. He went on to become one of the founders, for instance, of the Screenwriters Guild. But many of his leftist friends were uncomfortable with his unrelieved pessimism. West even tried to please them, and to put politics into *The Day of the Locust.* But it just didn't work. The original ending of the book was far more explicit in its politics than the version West finally sent to the printers. In that first version, Todd is taken to his friend's house, where they argue about class warfare. West wanted *The Day of the Locust* to be a Marxist morality play. He wanted to say that proletarian politics offered hope. But he decided against this ending. Ultimately he was saying "Nothing redeems, and there's no promise of redemption," Martin says. Black humor and unmitigated pessimism didn't become popular until the fifties, when the West revival began.

It is clear that West could most certainly be counted as the first Jewish writer in America to achieve entry into the ranks of the nation's great writers, even if Nathan Weinstein did change his name to the oh-so-English-sounding Nathanael West. Martin suggested to me that West's pessimism "probably had its source in his own personal sense of marginality as a Jew and a writer, but the nation was marginal too." His abandonment of his heritage without anything to replace it helped to mold this "complicated, bizarre, eccentric person," as retired UCLA Librarian Lawrence Clark Powell described him. He was uniquely attracted to the bizarre and absurd. He loved the story, which he would constantly retell, of the famous Hollywood mogul who had actually hired someone to wipe his behind. More than one critic has noted that although West derided Hollywood as a place for a real writer to be, Hollywood was bound to be the place where West's jaundiced view and taste for the extreme would make the most sense.

West's family had been well-to-do builders and craftsmen in their native Lithuania. When, like so many other millions of Russian Jews, they fled the Czar's pogroms, they proved quite adept at becoming builders in New York City. West was never outstanding academically, but by fudging his academic records he went to college and enjoyed the life of the pampered collegiate that Fitzgerald wrote about. The Depression, however, began in the late twenties for West's family. The Weinsteins lost nearly everything, and it was only because of the family's remaining business connections that West was able to get a job as a night clerk in a couple of New York hotels. Several of his broke writer friends from Greenwich Village had roofs over their heads only because of West. Dashiell Hammett, for instance, finished *The Maltese Falcon* because West sneaked him into a room. Yet during West's Parva-Sed days, Hammett, who was in a position to help West, lent him a little money but extracted a heavy emotional price for it. Among the writers indebted to West were Quentin Reynolds, Erskine Caldwell, and James T. Farrell.

West helped pay for a private publishing of his first novel, *The Dream Life of Balso Snell,* in 1931. He also rather light-heartedly changed his name for the occasion, inspired in his choice of a new name by Horace Greeley's saying "Go West, young man." His *Miss Lonelyhearts* was published in 1933 by the prestigious firm of Boni & Liveright. Unfortunately the prestigious firm went bankrupt a week before President Roosevelt declared a bank holiday, and the books hardly got to the bookstores. Not that anyone was buying them.

A year later, however, F. Scott Fitzgerald's *The*

Great Gatsby was reprinted by Modern Library. In his new introduction for it, Fitzgerald mentioned West as an up-and-coming talent. Later, when West applied for a grant from the Guggenheim Foundation, Fitzgerald, Malcolm Cowley, Edmund Wilson, and George S. Kaufman wrote letters of recommendation. However, the Guggenheim, in its wisdom, declined to sponsor West, although ironically enough, when Jay Martin wrote his biography of West he did it on a Guggenheim grant.

West wrote his third novel, *A Cool Million,* after his first visit to Hollywood in 1933. It didn't do well. He returned to L.A. in 1935 to make a living and write about Hollywood, but it wasn't until the beginning of 1936, after he had moved out of the Parva-Sed Apta, that he took a job. Then he began a modestly successful career as a screenwriter, which lasted the rest of his short life. West was, as was mentioned, pragmatic about screenwriting, and did not regard it as being very much different from hotel night-clerking. The difference was money—$50 a week versus $250, and finally, $350 a week. West worked at Republic Studios in Gower Gulch, off Sunset Boulevard. The studio was mainly known for making films no one ever remembered, and for the most part West's stuff was pretty much like everyone else's there.

During the time West was laid up at the Parva-Sed with his various ailments, another young writer whose first books had achieved critical acclaim but little commercial success, William Faulkner, was also desperate for work in Hollywood, and would have taken a job at fifty dollars a week. Both Faulkner and West made fairly good money later, in the studios; and they went hunting together in the Tulare marshes of the San Joaquin Valley or in the Santa Cruz area. Supposedly both enjoyed a passion for hunting and didn't bother talking about writing during their jaunts.

Fitzgerald and West met again in Hollywood—after the incident with the Guggenheim—and toward the end of both of their lives they became close. In April of 1939 West sent Fitzgerald galleys of *The Day of the Locust,* telling him how difficult it had been to write in between "working on westerns and cops and robbers." When the book came out that year, it sold fewer than fifteen hundred copies. It didn't even make back the paltry five-hundred-dollar advance West had been given.

West was not, of course, happy about this, but friends report he was becoming far less pessimistic because of his marriage in 1939 to Eileen McKenney, the "Eileen" of the popular book, *My Sister Eileen,* written by her sister Ruth. The couple purchased a handsome house, then only four years old, that still stands at 12706 Magnolia Boulevard in North Hollywood. Fitzgerald lived nearby in Encino with Sheila Graham. The two couples became very friendly, and were frequent visitors in each other's houses. The two men often showed and discussed works in progress.

Yet it was the timing of their two deaths that linked them in a startling way. Fitzgerald suffered his fatal heart attack on December 21, 1940. West and Eileen were on a hunting trip in Mexicali, but they may well have heard of his death. It was the following day that West, never a terribly attentive driver, plowed into another car at an intersection near El Centro. Eileen died before she got to the hospital, and West died shortly thereafter.

The newspapers wrote more about her death than his because of the current fame of *My Sister Eileen.* West was described, not as the author of four obscure novels, but as a lowly screen scenarist. A further irony was that the bodies of West and Fitzgerald ended up in the same mortuary in Los Angeles. Later, Fitzgerald's body was shipped to Baltimore, and Sheila Graham left Hollywood to go east on December 26 on the Santa Fe Super Chief. S.J. Perelman was aboard that same train, taking West's body home in a casket.

It was more than a decade before West was rediscovered, and it wasn't until Jay Martin published his *Nathanael West: The Art of His Life* in 1971 that much was known about him. Martin says he suspects that one of the effects of his book was to "diminish the mystery of West's life." Nonetheless, a virtual industry of West criticism has grown up and still prospers in academia. Martin also says West's works are still being discovered in other parts of the world—West was published for the first time in the Soviet Union two years ago.

To a limited extent West's work foreshadowed that of such Jewish writers as Philip Roth and Saul Bellow. To a great extent Joseph Heller's *Catch-22* was influenced by West's black humor and sense of the absurd.

When Jay Martin's biography of West appeared in England, such famous British critics as C.P. Snow and Anthony Burgess suggested that West had been a greater writer than either Faulkner or Hemingway. Even if this is hyperbole, it has made me look at the old Parva-Sed Apta with more than a little awe. It's made me look at all those old Hollywood apartment buildings with new respect, because of the tales they could tell, and in the case of the Parva-Sed (with some help from one Nathan Weinstein) did tell.

FOUR

Thomas Mann:
Faustus in the Palisades

I became obsessed with the twentieth century's most famous musical and literary controversy simply because one afternoon back in the '50s I was hit over the head with a viola case by the son of Germany's greatest living writer.

I was sitting with my mother in the back seat of the family Hillman Minx going south on Overland Avenue, and we had just cleared the hill on the way to Venice Boulevard. My father and Michael Mann, son of the Nobel Prize–winning German author Thomas Mann, were in the front seat. We were on our way to USC, where Michael and my mother were going to give one of the concerts broadcast every Sunday on radio station KFAC.

My mother, Yaltah Menuhin, is a pianist, and she and Michael had toured throughout Europe. Now another, bigger tour was lined up; but all that was about to end. For just as we came off the hill on Overland, Michael turned around, threw the viola case at me, and lunged at my mother with a knife he had been concealing. He cut her right about the eye. Then he jumped out of the car and ran.

Later, after a visit to the hospital where my mother needed to be stitched up, Katia Mann—Michael's mother and wife of the writer—called us in West Los Angeles. You have to understand that the Mann presence in our house was perennial in those days. For one thing, Michael spent a lot of time around our house on Pelham Avenue. I remember being awed at the quantities of cheap red wine he consumed many nights, and the earnestness with which he imbibed it; the more he drank, the more he sulked and scowled. I also know that my mother had been reaching the end of her rope with the Mann family, and this latest incident convinced her this was it.

Katia and, I presume, Thomas himself, were anxious to patch things up. Later, in fact, they were afraid my mother was going to sue them for the ruin of the upcoming world tour. My mother said she had no intention of suing; she just didn't want to have anything more to do with the Manns.

Katia began the conversation a little huffily, saying that my mother must have "done something to upset Michael," and added something to the effect that one should never upset a Mann. Katia said that what had happened to my mother was not such a big deal; he used to do that all the time to *her* when he was a child. My mother acidly replied that "a Mann had tried to kill a Menuhin," and she didn't want to have anything more to do with them. When Michael called her many years later to attempt a reconciliation, she again told him she did not wish to renew the friendship.

"That had been the way Katia gave in to the moods and demands of her husband, just as she did with the children," my mother said during a recent phone interview from London, where she now lives and concertizes. "There was this demonic force in Thomas Mann. He seemed to be very gentle and mild on the outside—he was always courteous with me—but anybody who wrote the things that he wrote was not just a gentle, melancholy mess after all."

In my mother's opinion—which, she is the first to admit, is far from objective—Mann was a highly overrated writer, even though some critics have called him the greatest writer of the century and *Doctor Faustus* his greatest work. To my mother, the fact that his books are so pessimistic and offer no hope of optimism invalidates them.

"He was like a Tolstoy, an idealist for the world, victimizing his family into sharing the life he felt was right. He considered himself the champion of freedom, but at home there was a lot of tyranny."

Thomas Mann was the most famous of the many famous refugees from Hitler's Germany who sought out the untroubled blue skies over Los Angeles, so far away from the Holocaust in Europe. Primarily because of the chamber music often played there, our front room on Pelham Avenue was one of the salons where they frequently gathered. It was a small, incestuous world, all these famous names in European literature and music in Los Angeles. Many of the greatest personalities, as well as egos, had come to L.A. to escape Hitler. Some were Jews, of course, but many, like Mann and Stravinsky, were not. Some were quite left-wing; others were conservative. Yet they clung together, mostly in desperation, for they did not sense then that Los Angeles had any great appreciation of their presence.

Among the results of all this were some rancorous arguments as well as warm social scenes. Undoubtedly, the most famous of the ideological and personal battles to hit the exile community occurred between Mann and Arnold Schoenberg over the publication of Mann's *Doctor Faustus*. It was a battle with literary, political and musical implications that have not been resolved to this day.

To my mother, however, the ideological battles weren't half so important as the reality of the individuals themselves. She tends to see things on individual rather than grandiose, ideological levels. To her, the whole Mann family reminded her of one of the elder Mann's novels. "No boundaries were set. There was no understanding of any normal, natural relationships," she said. She did not feel comfortable, for example, with Mann's fascination for the "homosexual thing" that was typical of the period in Germany before Hitler. "It was supposed to be a much higher form of love," she said, "than that of the normal bourgeois who married a woman and had children. It was a protest against convention."

Talking of the great debate over *Doctor Faustus* between Mann and Schoenberg, she says that she has sadly had to conclude that the exiles were "scarred in a way, damaged by their experience. They all demanded total loyalty from their worshippers. If you talked to them about anything they couldn't explain or that might throw a shadow on any of their ideas, they immediately reacted with the old Nazi idea of 'we're superior and you don't understand us.' I mean Nazi in the sense that one is supposed to accept the word of one who knows best, without any kind of protest. They never understood there was space for all of them. It was idol worship really," she says, adding that she believed the refugees were marked by a "mixture of melancholy, resentment and even a stain of the victimizers."

It is ironic that my mother never actually read *Doctor Faustus*, even though she sometimes saw its creator on a nearly daily basis, because Mann's great work addresses itself to the very things she does. She read other of his works, but not *Doctor Faustus*, which, ironically, he was actually working on when she first came in contact with the Manns. She knew, for instance, that Michael Mann, who was a member of the San Francisco Symphony when she first met him, was helping his father with the musical passages in *Doctor Faustus*, and that was a lot of help, for music is what the book is about.

Furthermore, one of the most powerful characters in *Doctor Faustus* is Nepomuk, or Echo, an angelic child who appears in the last pages of the book. When I was reading *Doctor Faustus* and came across Echo I had the odd feeling that I knew the lad. He seemed very familiar—I don't know if it was because Michael Mann's son, Thomas Mann's favorite nephew, was the model for Echo. "You remember Michael's son, who gave me the mumps that time, don't you?" my mother asked. "He was such a nice, quiet boy; today he is a theologian in Germany. I saw him not long ago in Zurich."

I must admit that, on listening to her recount all these things, I could see why I felt at least vicariously involved in the great battle between Schoenberg and Mann over *Doctor Faustus*, which occurred on our shores—quite literally our sun-drenched shores in the Pacific Palisades, where Mann lived at 1550 San Remo Drive.

At this point, it would probably be appropriate to mention that *Doctor Faustus* is the "biography of the composer Adrian Leverkuhn, as told by a friend," who is, not so incidentally, a parody Mann wrote on himself. *Doctor Faustus*, however, is much more than just a purported biography (the book is, after all, fiction). *Doctor Faustus* is the story of a great nation's descent into the maelstrom of total barbarity—what happened in Germany between her two great defeats in World War I and World War II.

Mann tells the story of his beloved nation's descent into bestiality by the parallel story of Leverkuhn, an avant-garde composer who, by the time *Doctor Faustus* was supposedly written, had achieved some degree of sanctification. Leverkuhn was conceived by Mann as the ultimate anti-Beethoven figure. Beethoven, of course, was Germany's greatest artist, the representative of hope, optimism and democracy. Leverkuhn was quite the opposite.

One of the last conversations Leverkuhn has with Zeitblom, the narrator who is supposed to be his friend, reveals the fullness of his misanthropy. He blurts out, "I find that it is not to be."

"What, Adrian, is not to be?" Zeitblom responds.

"The good and noble, what we call the human, although it is good, and noble. What human beings have fought for and stormed citadels, what the ecstatics exultantly announced—that is not to be. It will be taken back. I will take it back," replies Leverkuhn, pointing out that these were the things Beethoven had in mind in his great "Ode to Joy" in the Ninth Symphony.

In its various biographical details, the figure of Leverkuhn was not Mann's neighbor, Arnold Schoenberg, who lived not far away from the Pacific Palisades in Brentwood, at 116 N. Rockingham. Leverkuhn is more like the famed German philosopher Nietzsche, who died after a prolonged period of insanity brought on by syphilis, a disease Beethoven is believed to have suffered from as well. But the musical system that Leverkuhn invents as part of his deal with the devil, the system of musical composition that enables Leverkuhn to make the "artistic breakthrough" composers from the turn of the century were looking for, is almost wholly borrowed from Schoenberg. And this is where things got tricky between the two great exiles sequestered on Los Angeles's golden shores.

There could be little doubt that Leverkuhn was the inventor of the same method of "composing with twelve tones" as that of Schoenberg. After all, until Schoenberg, composers hadn't even considered inventing a system of composition in order to make music. Musicality was regarded as something innate; technique was primarily a tool for getting the music down on paper. Schoenberg, however, "constructed" music, using a mathematical system of his own devising. From the beginning, the results this system produced

were highly controversial. So when Mann had Leverkuhn invent a musical system, there could be little doubt about what system he was talking about.

"If I were Schoenberg with his esoteric musical theory and I sat down to read *Faustus,* I would be a little disturbed, too," declared Steve Willett, a former professor of literature at Northwestern University and a graduate of Los Angeles's own Occidental College. Willett is particularly interested in Mann and German literature, and he had long conversations on the subjects with Erich Heller, regarded as the foremost Mann authority in the world today.

Willett went on to say, "While Schoenberg could say that he and Leverkuhn were not the same, for Mann had indeed written burlesques of specific composers in previous books, I would see some rather serious implications in *Doctor Faustus.* Were I Schoenberg with my twelve-tone system, I wouldn't like at all the esthetics Mann had hooked me into."

Even though most of Schoenberg's increasingly strident objections to *Doctor Faustus* centered on what he called the theft of his intellectual property by Mann, Willett points out that more to the point is what Mann was saying the Leverkuhn-Schoenberg system represented. In fact, Michael Mann himself—who later quit music and became a professor of German at UC Berkeley—said he thought Schoenberg was really upset because of the political and historical implications his father was making.

Leverkuhn, after all, is hardly an attractive character. He is a man literally possessed by purgatory, a sickly man with demonic drives, whose musical system expressed and helped lay the ground for the triumph of the well-ordered barbarism that was Nazism. Leverkuhn's system creates a music that eschews melody and harmony in favor of a "collective polyphony" reminiscent of earlier times; Mann certainly must have been aware that the same sort of criticism had been leveled at Schoenberg's system as well.

Mann stoutly denied that Leverkuhn was Schoenberg, yet he inscribed a copy of *Doctor Faustus* to Schoenberg saying that he was "the real one." Furthermore, although Leverkuhn's life is in a few ways like Schoenberg's, Leverkuhn is one of the strangest characters in twentieth-century letters; in almost no place in the book is he given much of a physical presence. One hardly knows what he looks like; and that is as Mann intended. Leverkuhn was the embodiment of an *idea,* the great anti-Beethoven figure.

It is surely not coincidence that in 1908 Schoenberg wrote some music for poems by Stefan George for voice and piano. Schoenberg regarded this work as his great "breakthrough"—melody and harmony almost completely drowned out by atonality—and he believed that he had finally succeeded in his (and Leverkuhn's) claim of emancipating dissonance with his work. In *Doctor Faustus,* at about the same point in history, Leverkuhn completed his Brentano songs, and called it his "breakthrough" work.

Also, the whole background of Stefan George suggests the brutality of the intellectual satire Mann may have been committing on his neighbor and acquaintance. Stefan George, with whom Schoenberg was so enchanted, died in 1933. He is today regarded as the spiritual father of Nazism. Blood and uniforms, little boys dressed up in Greek robes, diabolical rites; these were among the things that excited this strange man. A lot of his poems were overwritten paeans to the beauty of various young men, for George was a rather flamboyant, decadent, aristocratic type of homosexual, whose poems didn't make much sense except to the Illuminati.

Like Schoenberg—and Leverkuhn—George was a dedicated member of the so-called avant-garde, which was always searching for a "higher order." George was proud and overly sensitive and no doubt felt very misunderstood. His inner vision was not meant for all mankind, as Beethoven and the poet Schiller had intended the "Ode to Joy" to be. George's work was done for an elect few, as was Schoenberg's. Schoen-

berg felt, in fact, that only his musical peers had a right to pass judgment on his works—and, interestingly enough, Schoenberg's music has continued to draw more enthusiasm in academic circles than among the regular crowd of music lovers.

Schoenberg felt that his music would find wide acceptance a few decades down the line. But this has not happened. What has happened is that he has achieved a kind of sainthood in contemporary music schools. There is Schoenberg Hall at UCLA, since he taught there. And there is Schoenberg Institute across town at USC. Yet to those who find that his compositions sound more like cacophony than music, it's a mystery why academics get so excited over Schoenberg. Steve Willett points out that the avant-garde has similarly suppressed the traditional narrative structure in literature, just as melody has been dismissed as "too sweet" in academia, where the avant-garde has become the status-quo. "The works which seem to be major landmarks in twentieth-century culture," Willett says, "are marked by what the devil gave Leverkuhn; an enthusiasm for evil, madness and mental disorder."

Although this commentary may seem strong, similar language has been used by others who are less than awestruck by Schoenberg. The great critic and writer, Louis Untermeyer, was reported to have left a performance of Schoenberg's famed "Pierrot Lunaire" harumphing, "Moonlight in the sickroom."

Although Schoenberg may have run in circles that provided the intellectual and artistic soil for the Third Reich that was later to emerge from post-World War I Germany and Austria, he himself was not loved by the Nazis. This was because he was born a Jew. He converted to Christianity in his youth, when Hitler gave him no choice, but he later rediscovered his Jewishness and fled Europe, ending up in Los Angeles with the likes of composers Stravinsky and Mario Castelnuovo-Tedesco, who dismissed Schoenberg's work as "composition by slide rule."

Ernest Gold, who came from Schoenberg's native Vienna and now lives in Pacific Palisades himself, told me that he regards Schoenberg as a second-rate talent who couldn't write a *good* melody, and so decided that music should have *no* melody. Gold has written both serious music and successful movie music, including the Oscar-winning score for *Exodus.* "Besides," says Gold, "look at his odd relationship with that Nazi, Hauer."

Joseph Matthias Hauer was a contemporary of Schoenberg's who also claimed to have invented the twelve-tone method. He and Schoenberg tried on more than one occasion to get together for the common cause of atonality. But they would usually fall out, primarily because even in the great cause of their esoteric innovations, Hauer couldn't bring himself to work side by side with a Jew.

Schoenberg was a notorious autocrat. Once when his wife was enjoying a knitting circle with some friends in the kitchen, Schoenberg told the women to stop because they were distracting him, when it would have made more sense for the great composer to have moved. But then Mann, apostle of Democracy, needed constant attention to his every whim from his wife Katia, too. "She would have killed the children so he could do his work undisturbed," Yaltah told me, adding that she was sick of the stridency of the old arguments that ran through the refugee community, and sicker yet of all the competing egos.

Katia Mann blamed the great flap between her husband and Schoenberg on Alma Mahler-Werfel, who had once been married to the composer Gustav Mahler. Katia said that the former Mrs. Mahler, then remarried to Franz Werfel (author of *The Song of Bernadette*), was malicious, mean, and drank too many sweet liqueurs. The Manns and the Werfels were much closer than the Manns and the Schoenbergs. Katia insisted that it was the former Mrs. Mahler who brought to Schoenberg's attention the whole Leverkuhn parallel. Katia wasn't overimpressed with the former Mrs. Mahler, although she said her husband was. "She was difficult to get along with," Katia wrote in her *Unwritten Memories,* "and she gave her former husband Gustav Mahler a very difficult time. She alienated him from all his friends and made him break off with his female admirers. Mahler died young. I think she was rather too much for his nervous system."

In those same memoirs, Katia also makes it clear that she wasn't much fonder of the Schoenbergs. But she was particularly appalled with the Schoenberg offspring, one of whom is now a judge in Beverly Hills. She said they were terribly "ill-behaved."

Katia also tells a fascinating story, during her diatribe against the family, about how Schoenberg died. Her point was that Schoenberg was not only an unpleasant man, but a superstitious man as well. It seems that Schoenberg had long been sure he was going to die on the thirteenth day of the month, so on July 13, 1951, Gertrud Schoenberg sat up with her husband, holding his hand, just as she had done on previous occasions when it was the thirteenth midnight of the month. She was worried about his nervousness because he was seventy-six and suffered from a heart condition. Nonetheless, on this July night it appeared that he had lived through another 13th, so Schoenberg went upstairs to bed while Mrs. Schoenberg, as was her custom, stayed downstairs in the kitchen to make him a hot drink. When she took his drink upstairs he was dead—and the clock upstairs in the bedroom was just turning midnight. She decided that the clock *downstairs* had killed him by being fast. When he had come upstairs by himself and seen it was actually still the 13th and not yet midnight, the shock had killed him on the spot, Gertrud reasoned.

In fairness to Schoenberg—some of whose critics have suggested that his interest in numerology showed that his system was more a system of metaphysics than the science of music he claimed it was – Mann was also fascinated by numerology. How else could he have written *Doctor Faustus*?

Doctor Faustus is not an easy book to read; it supposes a certain knowledge of music. The book has particularly intrigued musicians and musicologists alike, for Mann accomplished an amazing thing. The musical system, and indeed the musical works he created only in words, made such sense to people, it was as if they could hear them. In a very real sense, Schoenberg could be said to have accomplished not so very much more, because his music is still more talked about than listened to or played.

If Mann was parodying Schoenberg's intellectual system, he was attracted as well as repelled by it. In a sense, *Doctor Faustus* has an appearance of being "constructed." Mann rarely made up people and events; he almost always took them from real life. More than his powers of imaginative storytelling, Mann's greatness was in his perceptions and his ability to synthesize. Especially in *Doctor Faustus,* he saw where the patterns of culture and history came together. His writing sometimes seemed musical, as if his works had melodies and harmonies, yet he was himself only an amateur pianist. His son was the only real musician in the family.

The great controversy among the two exiles did not stay exclusively on the lovely, smogless shores of Los Angeles long. As the *Saturday Review* noted in 1949, "*Doctor Faustus* has occasioned one of the notable literary controversies of our time."

Schoenberg complained in a letter to the *Saturday Review* that Mann had stolen his "intellectual property" in order to lend "the hero of his book qualities a hero needs to arouse people's interest." He went on to state that Mann had done this "without my permission and even without my knowledge." Schoenberg then blamed a former acquaintance, a musicologist and philosopher, Theodor Wisengrund-Adorno, who

had studied the system. In fact, Schoenberg was right: Mann had consulted Wisengrund-Adorno at some length in the writing of *Doctor Faustus*.

Schoenberg and Wisengrund-Adorno had had some sort of falling-out; no one was sure just what caused it. However, it was also known in L.A.'s exile community during the writing of *Doctor Faustus* that Mann was working on a novel that borrowed heavily from Schoenberg's musical system. In fact, once when Mann and Schoenberg were together at a barbecue at the Werfels', Mann pumped the composer for musical and biographical information.

Schoenberg's letter to the *Saturday Review* further complained that Mann's dedication of *Doctor Faustus* had read, in German, "To A. Schoenberg, the real one." Schoenberg said he took this to mean that Leverkuhn "was an impersonation of myself." He pointed out that he was not a lunatic, "and I have never acquired the disease from which this insanity stems. I consider this an insult." Schoenberg further alleged that when Mann was confronted with evidence indicating that he had borrowed wholesale from his neighbor, he replied, "Oh, does one notice that? Then perhaps Mr. Schoenberg will be angry?"

Mann's reply to Schoenberg was to say he was "both astonished and grieved." He pointed out that the two had already exchanged letters on the subject, and he thought the composer had been mollified with the note penned at the end of the English edition of *Doctor Faustus* which more or less admitted that Schoenberg and not the fictional Leverkuhn was the inventor of the twelve-tone system.

Mann suggested that Schoenberg had never read the book, that he knew it only through "the gossip of meddling scandal-mongers." He argued that he was certainly not trying to steal Schoenberg's system, which everybody knew Schoenberg had invented. Mann then tried to explain what he meant by his inscription to "the real one." He was trying to say to

Schoenberg, "Not Leverkuhn is the hero of this musical era; you are its hero." He protested that his respect for Schoenberg was profound, that he thought of Schoenberg as a "bold and uncompromising artist." He stated flatly: "The idea that Adrian Leverkuhn is Schoenberg, that the figure is a portrait of him, is so utterly absurd that I scarcely know what to say about it."

Mann pointed out that, in many details, Leverkuhn's life was closest to Nietzsche's, and to some extent his own. He suggested that Schoenberg should have accepted his book with "a satisfied smile" that "testifies to his tremendous influence on the musical culture of the era" rather than regarding *Doctor Faustus* as a "rape and an insult." Said Mann, with perhaps only a hint of courtly sarcasm: Schoenberg should "rise above the bitterness and suspicion and that he may find peace in the assurance of his greatness and glory."

Perhaps Mann's cordiality was, in part, fully serious. It seemed that the more he protested that he did not want to become Schoenberg's enemy, the more the composer was galled, and rallied his supporters to the fight. After all, they *had* been friends. Mann had complimented Schoenberg once on what good coffee he made—something very important to the Viennese. And Schoenberg had dedicated a work to Mann. Mann had even given Schoenberg a copy of his *Magic Mountain* with the inscription, "From somebody who also tries to build music—Thomas Mann."

Bombs are falling on a defeated Nazi Germany as *Doctor Faustus* ends, and it is symbolic that Leverkuhn is in an advanced state of syphilitic madness. Schoenberg and Stefan George were in their heyday long before Nazi Germany arose. Yet Mann traces the rise of fascism from their milieu.

Mann's message is not a simple one, however. He is not saying that everything avant-garde was bad. To Schoenberg and others, at the turn of the century in Germany and Austria, it appeared that music had reached a dead end—in fact, not just music, but all of the arts. Wagner had pushed melodies and harmonies to such a point that he had left nothing for composers who followed him. Thus, much of the music after Wagner does seem like parody. Sometimes, as in the compositions of Hindemith, the form became ever more elegant and complex. Mahler struck many people as only a second-rate Wagner. Compared with the works of Beethoven, the first romantic, who emphasized so many great and rich melodies, music seemed to have little content any more. The new composers were using the old forms and saying nothing new. Much of their music seemed hollow.

What to do? This was the question that concerned artists at the turn of the century and into the Weimar Republic. The avant-garde believed that the solution was to change the form of music, not to find new content. Part of the deal the devil makes with Leverkuhn is this promise: "You will lead the way, you will strike up the march of the future, the lads will swear by your name, who, thanks to your madness will no longer need to be mad."

The Leverkuhn system took music-making away from individual expression and returned it to the tribal polyphony of earlier, more barbaric times. Composers would no longer be able to make music that had their own distinctive melodies and harmonies if Leverkuhn's system triumphed. The clear suggestion was that composing music by his system was a very totalitarian thing. Steve Willett insists that the whole point of Leverkuhn is that he represents pure expression of feeling, unconscious tribal feeling, untroubled by logic or reason, the peculiarly human qualities that ultimately are our only improvement over other animals on this globe. As Willett says this, however, he points out that others might have a different interpretation. "You understand," he says, "you are getting yourself into this vortex, this quicksand of Faustus criticism, which is endless."

The matter was not just of academic interest to me.

After all, I had been initiated into this whole matter of *Doctor Faustus,* an incredibly ambitious work that ties culture and history together, with a hit on the head. The critics have been arguing ever since the book was published about just how well Mann connected the two. Certainly the most surprising thing about this most ambitious and profound of twentieth-century works is that it was rooted in a saga that unfolded on Los Angeles's golden shores as well as in the musty halls of European culture.

You can see that the work Thomas Mann created here was indeed a major event in literary and musical history; so was the saga of his battle with his neighbor over it, for it revealed at least part of what Mann was talking about. I must admit I disagree with my mother about the historical importance of Thomas Mann. Her preference in writers tends toward Willa Cather, the great American author who was known by my mother as "Aunt Willa."

My mother spent a lot of time with Willa Cather as a child, and perhaps that is where she acquired her dislike for the playwright Eugene O'Neill. O'Neill, like Mann, was pessimistic in the extreme. Willa Cather usually struck notes of optimism as well as despair in her writing.

The critics have long argued about the effect of Los Angeles on Mann. Usually, musicians fare better in exile than writers. Writers need to read and hear their native language; they need their audiences and their familiar surroundings to write about. Mann, however, was famous enough so that he could try to transcend the lack of these things in Los Angeles.

Some have said that *Doctor Faustus* turned out all the better for Mann's being in exile in Los Angeles. He was alone and cut off. He worried about his homeland and hated it at the same time. He was not at all comfortable among the natives of Los Angeles, any

more than *any* of the exiles were. That's why they clung together so tenaciously. Yet against adversity and ill health (Mann was sixty-six when he came to Los Angeles in 1941), Steve Willett asserts, Mann's German developed a purer, deeper, and perhaps more classical turn, which is part of the reason *Doctor Faustus* is regarded as his masterpiece.

Mann was not himself avant-garde, either in his own art or in his personal taste. *Doctor Faustus* may have been intricate at times, but it had a traditional narrative form. Mann far preferred the late romantics, such as Wagner, to the likes of Schoenberg.

Here is how the seclusion in L.A. might have helped: First of all, the Pacific reminded everyone of the Mediterranean coast. A source of obscenely easy money in the Hollywood dream factories was close by.

In the days before Hitler demolished all of Europe by war, great artists used to seek out places where they could have the seclusion to work and also to relax in the company of each other. Lakeside resorts in the Alps or seaside Mediterranean villas were the favorites. During the '30s, for instance, a rural region, Sils-Maria in the Swiss Alps, was popular. The local peasants supplied fresh milk and cheese to the artists in their rented farmhouse retreats for serious discussion of the great philosophical and political passions then sweeping the globe.

Surely if Mann had not come to L.A. and had not had Schoenberg as a neighbor and friend, he would not have written *Doctor Faustus.* And I'm absolutely sure that had Michael not hit me over the head with his viola case southbound on Overland Avenue, I would never have gotten around to reading Thomas Mann at all, and I might have missed the book some critics have hailed as the greatest novel of the twentieth century. It was written in Los Angeles.

FIVE

Aldous Huxley's Strange Passage to the West

Once when a reporter asked Aldous Huxley why he had lived the last third of his life in the Los Angeles area, the great English writer replied he had merely stopped there on his way to India and ended up staying because of "inertia and apathy."

I remember counting myself lucky to be an L.A. resident the day I shook hands with the great man not too long before Huxley's death on November 22, 1963, the same day President Kennedy was assassinated. Upon the same occasion I also met Laura, Huxley's second wife, not realizing, of course, that nearly two decades later she would once again cause me to remember and contemplate the ghost of that tall willowy man, by getting me involved in a strange adventure out in the Mojave Desert.

On the second occasion, when I met only Huxley's widow, I was told by my uncle, Yehudi Menuhin, to put myself in the good hands of Laura Huxley. Yehudi had played the Bach Chaconne on his fiddle at the December 17, 1963 Memorial Gathering for Aldous in London. Yehudi had been very close to both Aldous and Laura, and it was because of Yehudi, of course, that I had been privileged to shake Huxley's hand so many years previously.

Yehudi remained on close terms with Laura, if for no other reason than because both he and Laura had been prodigy violinists as children. Also, Laura had dedicated her life to carrying on the mystical prescriptions by which her husband wanted ultimately to be remembered. My instructions from Yehudi were to put my life in Laura's hands, and she supposedly would mold me according to Huxleyan principals. I agreed, only after Yehudi insisted, that I would meet a yoga teacher through the kind offices of his good friend Laura.

Thus, I spent several evenings engaged in some interesting conversations with Laura after Yehudi left town. But I had to admit to her I really did not want to study yoga, that I had only said I would to humor my uncle. Yehudi had been very generous with his time and efforts when I wrote my first book, *The Menuhins: A Family Odyssey.* I agreed to meet the yoga teacher she knew, and so on one of my visits to Mrs. Huxley I met the yoga teacher, Janice Seaman.

Ms. Seaman was an interesting woman and a fine yoga teacher, I'm sure, but I never did find out. Instead, through Laura and her good friend Janice, I got involved in an arduous and rather terrifying story about the violent death in the Mojave Desert of the world-famous animal trainer Ted Derby. Derby had been despised by some of his Mojave Desert neighbors because of his menagerie of wild animals.

It was not just coincidence, I'm sure, that a few weeks before Yehudi entrusted me to the care of Aldous Huxley's widow, Huxley himself had been the topic of a curious discussion. It started early one evening and ran well into the next morning in the Denny's coffee shop on Highway 14, where the high desert starts, just past the last outpost of Saugus.

Huxley lived in the high desert throughout most of World War II. Although the landscape north of the San Gabriel Mountains is quite different than the city south of the mountain range, both are in Los Angeles County. Usually one does not think of L.A.'s cultural history as coming from the area north of the L.A. basin, but at the end of World War II Huxley wrote *Ape & Essence,* a novel about L.A. in the year 2018. It was far more grim than his more famous novel, *Brave New World.*

At the Denny's coffee shop on the edge of the desert we—my wife Nigey Lennon and I, and Don Van Vliet, best known as the rock-and-roll cult hero Captain Beefheart—talked of many things, finally leading up to a possibly apocryphal Beefheart story about Huxley. We had been discussing drugs, the '60s, and the high desert. Beefheart was talking about how people who live in the desert (where he was reared) are often far more eccentric than those who live on the other side of the San Gabriels.

Once, as a young lad growing up in the desert, Beefheart had a part-time job selling Electrolux vacuum cleaners in Pearblossom, which wasn't too far from Llano and Wrightwood, the desert communities Huxley lived near. Beefheart explained that it was known that the famous author lived in the desert, so when a tall, gangly customer came into the store where Beefheart was working, Beefheart recognized him immediately.

Van Vliet remembered being impressed by how

down-to-earth Huxley was. Huxley explained that his wife Maria (for Huxley's first wife did not die until the mid-50s) had sent him out to look for a vacuum cleaner. Huxley asked Van Vliet if he could recommend one. Since Beefheart was selling Electroluxes, it was, of course, an Electrolux Huxley purchased. Then they talked a bit, according to Beefheart.

It is quite likely that this was during the period when Huxley was writing *Ape & Essence,* in which case the great author must have been under the spell of some darkly powerful ruminations there in the high desert. During the conversation at Denny's, Beefheart said that Huxley had seemed to him a man who was looking for something, that he was an eccentric among the eccentrics who inhabit the desert. It is no doubt significant that Huxley described L.A. in that gloomy work created on the high desert as "the world's largest oasis," for it was as if he were viewing L.A. from the perspective of the desert.

I know that during some of the scarier moments of investigating the Derby story, in which Laura had involved me, I was coming to see the desert as a terribly strange and hostile place. The Derby tale was about the unsuccessful attempt to save Derby's menagerie of bears, tigers, birds, big cats and wolves, to mention just a few of his beasts, from the odd humans in the Mojave. It was a story right out of the tradition of *Ape & Essence.*

I had been a member of the '60s generation so deeply affected by Huxley's psychedelic experiences, which came after he left the high desert. But since then I had grown rather disillusioned about druggie mysticism, or indeed any mysticism. I sometimes found myself pondering the fact that I had been sent to Huxley's widow to set my life straight with mysticism, and instead found myself involved in a strange, almost cabalistic tale involving murder and other base human doings.

The first time Huxley saw Los Angeles was on a quick trip through in 1926. At the time, he dismissed the place as hopelessly uncivilized. Six years later Huxley published his famous *Brave New World,* the first of three utopian novels he would write. *Brave New World* was published in England in 1932, but Huxley's two other utopian novels, *Ape & Essence* and *Island,* were written during his twenty-four years in the Southland.

Although Huxley wrote scores of novels and books of essays, these three books show quite clearly the logic of his life. *Brave New World* was the end of his first period, during which Huxley established himself as a writer of great intelligence and graceful style. His early works, such as *Crome Yellow* and *Antic Hay,* had a tone of amused bewilderment with the human condition; the release of the writer's pain came in an outrageous, almost scatological, sense of humor. But his disillusionment with technology in *Brave New World* was the last of his good-natured, British works. *Ape & Essence* would mark the end of Huxley's second period, for its pessimism was extreme. It made *Brave New World* (and George Orwell's *1984*) seem like a picnic by comparison.

Aldous was from the most famous literary and scientific family in England. He and his brother, Sir Julian, were grandsons of Thomas Henry Huxley, the famed agnostic and the scientific colleague of Charles Darwin. Yet Aldous began showing a mystical if not a religious bent as early as 1936, in his *Eyeless in Gaza.* The year after, Huxley took his first wife Maria and their son Matthew and left Europe. As he became more and more a part of the Southern California landscape—especially after the *Ape & Essence* period—he became more and more mystical, with results that were controversial to his reputation.

Later in life it was almost as if he were disavowing his past. In the post-Victorian period in England, Huxley had been one of the bright, cynical, witty and properly rational young literary figures. But as the drift in world events seemed more and more to point inevitably in the direction of yet another, terrible world war, he became more and more the hopeless pacifist.

Huxley's strengths and weaknesses as a writer both came out of his Olympian view of things. Few of Huxley's characters ever seem to hold nine-to-five jobs, or worry about ordinary things like money. They are mostly successful in their careers. Perhaps this was to be expected in one from such an intellectually elite family. But perhaps some of his aloofness may also have been traceable to his near-blindness. He lost his eyesight in 1910, at 16 years, possibly because of inadequate if not incompetent medical care in school. He had enormous enthusiasm later in life, especially in California, for such unorthodox medical treatments as homeopathy, as well as the Bates Method, which claimed that eyesight could be improved through exercise, without the use of glasses.

There was always a controversy about how well Huxley could see. His most strident and uncritical admirers told many stories showing that he really could see quite well. Others were less convinced that Huxley had solved his vision problems as well as he thought he had. My own impression was that he was practically blind. Yet one of the reasons he loved the high desert and lived there for much of the Second World War was that he had an incredible eye for detail of flora and fauna. And he was able to drive on back dirt roads in the desert without known mishap. His wide knowledge of nature stood him in good stead during his many hikes and drives in the desert.

His growing mysticism, no doubt, also drew him to the desert. He was partial to the Eastern as opposed to the Western religious view of nature. Huxley felt that when man tries to dominate nature, it tolerates the intrusion only for so long before it rebels.

In Europe, Huxley had not been known as a man who had any great attachment to one place. He may have been somewhat fond of Italy, but mostly he liked to travel, and he was a fine travel writer. Still, when Huxley left Europe with his family there was little sense that he might be going for good.

The primary reason for Huxley's visit to the United States was to see Frieda Lawrence in Taos, New Mexico. She was the widow of D.H. Lawrence, and Lawrence and Huxley had been closely allied through different periods of their lives. There was something of the British gentleman in the additional reasons Huxley gave for his visit to America. He said, for instance, that he wanted to find a good college for his son in the United States. He was also interested in the unusual educational and psychological experimentation then going on in the U.S. that was not happening in Europe, he said.

The Huxleys stayed with Frieda in Taos for a few months, while Huxley finished *Ends & Means* there. Although the New Mexico landscape was astonishing and beautiful to Huxley, he said he did not enjoy it. He found the landscape alien and somehow "hostile to man." Huxley was not known to have had the same reaction to the Mojave—if he did, it may have been on the subconscious level. Maybe that had something to do with the extreme pessimism of *Ape & Essence*.

The next stop after New Mexico was Los Angeles. Huxley wasn't necessarily planning on staying when he rented an apartment here in 1937. But soon there was a whirl of things to keep him here. For one, there was his good friend from England, Gerald Heard, the mystic. Huxley and Heard hit the lecture circuit together. Huxley also made it clear that he was willing to entertain fantastic offers from Hollywood, which did, in fact, start coming his way.

During his first years in the Southland, Huxley did not live long in any one place. He moved around, from West Hollywood to the Pacific Palisades to Beverly Hills. But he fell in with good and entertaining company—people who'd do crazy things like have picnics on the bottom of the Los Angeles River or outdoor parties at The Farmer's Market.

Some of his friends and acquaintances included authors Christopher Isherwood and Anita Loos (*Gentlemen Prefer Blondes*), Edwin Hubble, the Mt. Wilson astronomer who was an early proponent of the expanding universe theory, the Great Garbo, and Charles Chaplin. Upton Sinclair was sometimes part of the circle, and the composer Igor Stravinsky was also very close to Huxley.

Huxley accomplished some good work in the movie studios, for which he was indeed well paid. He adapted such classics as *Pride and Prejudice* and *Jane Eyre*. He wrote the script for *Madam Curie*. And the movie *A Woman's Vengeance* was made from his own short story, "The Gioconda Smile."

Huxley's relationship to Los Angeles was curious. On the one hand he was appalled by the vacuity on the faces of the natives he saw riding on a department store escalator; on the other hand he was genuinely attracted by the cheap, fantastic, glimmering lifestyle of the area. He lived for a while in a house in the Pacific Palisades, rented from a man who had painted rather tasteless orgy scenes on the walls, which seemed to amuse Huxley somewhat. He was appalled, however, when he saw his first small towns in the Southland on the drive in from New Mexico. What bothered him was that so few of the towns had monuments or outdoor cafes with terraces.

He discovered that the research library at UCLA was second to none. Former UCLA Librarian Lawrence Clark Powell remembered Huxley as a courteous, distinctive, curious and amiable man, often stopping his labors at the card catalog to sign a student autograph.

In 1939 Huxley published the first of the two novels he wrote that had a Southern California setting. *After Many A Summer Dies the Swan* was a good novel, but that year also saw the publication of some other great California novels, Powell points out—there were *The Grapes of Wrath*, *The Big Sleep*, and *The Day of the Locust*.

After Many A Summer Dies the Swan was modeled on California's then most famous citizen, newspaper tycoon William Randolph Hearst. You might remember that a young filmmaker-actor named Orson Welles was making his immortal *Citizen Kane*, also based on Hearst, that year. The plot revolved around Kane's desire for immortality. The book, of course, was full of satire on Hollywood and included in its scenery a castle like Hearst's San Simeon—only instead of being located in California's midcoastal region, it was set in the San Fernando Valley.

Huxley spent three or four good years on the West Side, near the Pacific Ocean, before moving to the high desert behind the San Gabriel Mountains. Even in those pre-war days, there were hints of the smog that was to come to L.A., and part of the reason the Huxleys first thought of living in the desert was that the air was clean and dry there. They thought this would be good for Huxley's eyesight as well as for Maria's lung problems.

They moved to the Mojave Desert in 1942, to a place near the desert town of Llano. The heat in the summer was unbearable. Water shortages were regular events. Electricity was far from reliable. The "shack" the Huxleys purchased was constantly being worked on, and was makeshift at best. Huxley's study had a canvas ceiling propped up by a pole, for instance. When Christopher Isherwood came visiting, he remembered Maria Huxley asking him to read by candlelight because if he turned on the electric light, that would start up the noisy gas-engine generator outside.

Perhaps much of the grimness of *Ape & Essence* may have come from the fact that life on the high desert was sometimes too much seclusion, too much the joys of nature. During the war Huxley's royalty checks from England were gone, and gas, tires and spare parts were hard to come by. Eventually he would have to abandon the desert because he was finding more and more of his income in the studios. What is for sure is that no city ever had a more gloomy prophecy created for it than Huxley created for L.A. in that book written primarily in the Mojave.

Yet Huxley loved the desert. He loved the poplars and the Joshua trees, the flowers and rattlesnakes. In 1945 the Huxleys moved from Llano to Wrightwood, further up the mountains. A landscape of pinewood and sagebrush, which Huxley turned out to be terribly allergic to, surrounded them. A raccoon adopted Huxley, and it would come out of the hills every night to be fed. Huxley even reported meeting a bear on one of his walks at Wrightwood.

The move to Wrightwood came the year the atom bomb was tested and subsequently dropped on two Japanese cities. After the horrors of the Second World War in Europe, where Huxley still had many friends and relatives, the Nuclear Age thoroughly horrified him. In 1945 he wrote a friend, "Thank God we are to have peace soon," but went on to say that he thought it would be a disquieting peace at best, since "atomic bombs would be hanging overhead."

National states armed by science with superhuman military power always remind me of Swift's description of Gulliver being carried up on the roof of the King of Brobdingnag's palace by a gigantic monkey: reason, human decency and spirituality, which are strictly individual matters, find themselves in the clutches of the collective will, which has the mentality of a delinquent boy of fourteen in conjunction with the physical power of God.

The terrible pessimism that began to clutch Huxley from the late 1940s until the time in the 1950s when he discovered psychedelics dates from the advent of the atom bomb. He began *Ape & Essence* at his Wrightwood home in 1947. The idea for the book was to be that of a "post-atomic-war society in which the chief effect of the gamma radiation had been to produce a race of men and women who don't make love all the year around, but have a brief mating season. The effect of this on politics, religion, ethics, etc. would be something very interesting and amusing to work out," Huxley told Anita Loos.

Ape & Essence is not an easy novel to call amusing, unless, of course, one is amused by torture, brutality, degradation and other unspeakable horrors. Huxley wrote *Ape & Essence* with his considerable wit and satire, however, so it is not totally without humor.

On the 22nd of February, 1948, Huxley walked into the kitchen at Wrightwood and told his wife he thought he had finished the book. The survivors in the book were mutants. The original inhabitants of L.A. had been killed long ago, in "those three bright summer days" of the Third World War. The physical city still stood; the wars had not scored a direct hit on L.A., but the radiation had destroyed most of the crops as well as finishing off the human population. Thus the handful of mutants, a few thousands at best, lived in and among various familiar Southern California landmarks—the County Museum and Coliseum in Exposition Park, Pershing Square and the Biltmore Hotel across the way, USC and UCLA and so on. The outlying neighborhoods were still there too, only they were not inhabited. The gas stations were rusting.

The community center of the mutant survivors of L.A. was in Pershing Square. The mutants were oddly dressed, because their clothes came from corpses dug up from nearby graveyards. They drank from skulls of the corpses, which had been fashioned into cups. Heat for the communal baking ovens in Pershing Square was provided by burning the books from the nearby public library. Water was carried in goatskins to be stored in earthenware jars kept in Pershing Square. Between "two rusty posts hung the carcass of a newly slaughtered ox and in a cloud of flies a man was cleaning out the entrails."

Across the way from this charming scene in Pershing Square was the mutants' temple — in the old Biltmore Hotel. In the book, the clergy lived there, chief of whom was "His Eminence the Arch-Vicar of Belial, Lord of the Earth, Primate of California, Servant of the Proletariat, Bishop of Hollywood." His aides included the "Patriarch of Pasadena" and the "Three-Horned Inquisitor."

The main event of the year, which was held in the Biltmore, was a two-week period of wild, enforced, orgiastic copulating, for sex was outlawed the rest of the year. The woman wore flaps over strategic parts of their bodies that had the word "No" emblazoned on them. Nine months after the orgy there was a corollary event: Belial Day, a mass, sacrificial slaughter of the deformed offspring born from the main event. Women were called vessels to signify their uncleanness. In the book, most of the children the vessels had were offered to the sacrificial fires of Belial Day.

Unlike other European writers who lived in L.A., Huxley did not leave the Southland after the Holocaust in Europe was over. But in 1949 he did abandon the desert and moved to 740 N. Kings Road in L.A. No doubt the fact of his proximity helped direct the attention of young intellectuals to his work. *Ape & Essence* was an especially popular book on Southland university and college campuses during the early '50s. In 1952 *The Devils of Loudon* was published, from which Ken Russell would later make the movie, *The Devils.* Not long thereafter, Huxley began dabbling with psychedelics because he found the chemical substances gave life to his admittedly intellectual mystical ideas. His *Doors of Perception* and *Heaven and Hell* in the mid-fifties made Huxley a major influence in his adopted town during the '60s with the psychedelic set.

Huxley was also active, with Christopher Isherwood and his friend Gerald Heard, in the Vedanta Society of Southern California. But it was the psychedelics that seemed to make Huxley a somewhat happier man than he might have been during the last part of his life.

After the death of his first wife, Maria, in 1955, Huxley did not produce much literature of lasting value. He seems to have been much less pessimistic, however, and his life with his new wife Laura saw him veer more and more in mystical directions. His last novel, *Island,* the manuscript of which was saved from the clutches of a fire which destroyed one of his homes in the Hollywood Hills, was his optimistic work. Here he attempted to demonstrate how human life could be lived ideally. Unfortunately, many critics and readers found it rather dull, because in it the customary Huxley critical faculty seemed to have been suspended.

Although Huxley gave L.A. some fine literary presents, topped by *Ape & Essence,* he remained ever the Englishman. It is fitting to note that he himself, when hearing a recording of his voice, commented on how terribly English-sounding he remained, despite living in the physical and intellectual desert of Southern California.

Jack London
May Have Slept Here

I t's been nearly twenty years since a friend who lived near Melrose and Wilton in Hollywood introduced me to one of the neighborhood's—dare I say the city's?—best-kept secrets. In an obscure alleyway called La Vista Court I caught my first glimpse of one of the most unusual-looking residences you'd ever hope to see. On its front, cast in the same plaster as was the house, was a bas-relief portrait of my favorite writer, Jack London. Beneath the portrait was the enameled inscription, "Jack London slept here."

For a couple of years my friend and I used to walk past the place and talk about it and about Jack London, and wonder what the history of the place was. Then, in the mid-'60s, I got my first newspaper job in Pismo Beach, nearly two hundred miles north of Los Angeles. On the last night before I left town, I decided to knock on the door of the house and find out what it was all about.

The man who came to the door was not at all upset at my interest in his place. His name was Robert Gary and he invited me up the narrow stairs to a second-floor apartment. This was the main apartment of London House, Gary explained, and he lived in it. He was also the landlord of four other apartments in the building. Gary's apartment had a two-story-high ceiling, capped off by a large skylight. There was also another set of narrow stairs going from his apartment to a third-story penthouse bedroom that towers over the other buildings on La Vista Court; you can clearly pick out London House from nearby Wilton because of the third story.

That first night, Gary and I talked late into the night, discussing Jack London as well as a number of other things. But Gary insisted that he did not want his house to be written about. Although the place was historical, he also lived in it. I remember going away from the house feeling that I had been lucky to have discovered London House, which nobody had ever written about. I spent the rest of the decade as a wandering newspaperman, more in the northern part of the state than the southern. When I eventually resettled in Los Angeles, it was not long before I was showing my friends the front of London House in La Vista Court in Hollywood every time I got a chance. If I couldn't write about it, by God, I was still going to make people aware of an unexpected piece of Los Angeles literary history – namely that the great Jack London, who was known as a Northern Californian writer, had also been something of an Angeleno.

Over the years I avoided knocking on the door of London House to talk with Gary, but I noticed that London House was looking more and more down on its uppers than it should have. The bas-relief of London had been knocked a little askew, whether by earthquakes or just plain settling I didn't know. The blue-enameled "Jack London slept here" sign that had so intrigued me at first was gone. A car had knocked another bas-relief sculpture of a sailing ship off the front of the house, although most of the various satyrs and nymphs adorning the house seemed to have withstood the ravages of time. The ship's lantern on the second floor seemed less red than it had been, and part of the block-and-tackle over the large two-part barn door on the second-floor apartment had come down. The stucco looked decidedly shabbier and even the external redwood pegs between the floor and ceiling seemed to be aging poorly.

On a hunch, I recently knocked on the door again. Gary wasn't there but I made arrangements to see him again. As it turned out, Gary remembered me. And as I suspected, he was now in a worse position than he'd been in the first time I met him. At present, although he's been pouring a good part of his salary into keeping up the house, it is needing more and more work all the time. Ultimately the place is going to require massive rebuilding, maybe fifty thousand dollars' worth, says Gary. It needs an entirely new foundation, for instance. Gary explained that he has been trying to do the work because he loves the place and thinks it has great historical importance, but none of this is easy. For the last four years, the Internal Revenue Service has called him in every year, demanding that he explain his rebuilding. "They don't care if it's an historic house; my economics just don't fit their computers. They think I take in too little income for the amount I'm spending on it," he says a bit ruefully. "If this were just a piece of real estate I guess that would be true," he adds.

Here I should explain that in the fifteen years between my two visits to the inside of the London House, the details of its history had taken on the warm, indistinct glow of a fantasy – most of it going back, I think, to the intriguing blue enamel sign that said "Jack London slept here." This fantasy was partly based on what I thought I had remembered during my first visit with Gary in the mid-'60s. I think Gary himself had subsequently learned more about the house than he had known on the occasion of my first visit.

Throughout most of the '70s, I showed many people the square, three-story structure that stands tall and looks so much different than anything else in the neighborhood. And I told them what I believed to be the information I had gotten from Gary on my first visit. I always said that the house dated back to 1870 or so. No one who ever saw the place doubted that it had to be at least a hundred years old. I had remembered Gary saying that London House was originally the ranch house of a cattle ranch that extended from Hollywood past where City Hall is now, in downtown L.A. Jack London—or so the story went—would come to this ranch house, which had been renamed in his honor by the friend who now owned the ranch, to buy livestock for his own Valley of the Moon ranch fifty miles north of San Francisco.

My impression, in other words, was that the London House had a noble and untold past as a sort of Bohemia South. I imagined great scenes occurring at the London House, where London and his companion George Sterling and other such greats got together for extended conversations. Over those fifteen years, I had often thought of the one piece of evidence that really linked London House to this imaginary Bohemia South: an inscription, on an inside wall of Gary's apartment, from Sterling, who was famous in his own right as a California poet as well as being London's close friend.

Like many writers since London, I first felt the call to the literary arts after reading his great, autobiographical *Martin Eden*. It was, of course, *The Call of the Wild* which first brought Jack London fame and fortune right after the turn of the century. He became the most successful and popular writer the world had ever seen, the Skid Row bestseller who was far bigger in his day than any movie or rock star has been since.

He was also the bastard son of an eccentric spiritualist and an itinerant Irish astrologer and writer. London's harsh childhood was spent in the slums of Oakland and environs, and sometimes in the nearby countryside on farms. It was a childhood of poverty and defeat. By the time he was ten years of age, he was working nineteen-hour days in waterfront factories to help support his family. By the time he was out of his teens, he had been king of the San Francisco Bay oyster pirates, a sailor around the world, an adventurer to the Yukon, a hobo, a famed revolutionary socialist, an alcoholic, and, most of all, a writer.

There is no more compelling version of a writer's trials and tribulations than those described in *Martin Eden:* cranking out his manuscripts, spending his last few cents on postage rather than food, seeing each day's mail bring more and more rejection slips. After a while he replaced his wallpaper with rejection notices. Yet when London struck it big, during the few short years that remained of his life, he had produced more than fifty books as well as countless articles and short stories. Not only did he write the greatest adventure stories, but he also produced such powerful social protest works as *People of the Abyss, The Iron Heel,* and *South of the Slot.*

The last years of London's life were spent on Glen Ellen, his ranch in the Valley of the Moon north of San Francisco. The hobos and sailors and drifters and criminals, working men, and hangers-on he had met in his world travels knew they were always welcome at Glen Ellen. London was a generous man and he spent money on anyone who happened to be around him. It is said that Glen Ellen typically had as many as five hundred visitors in a day. Furthermore, if a man wanted a job at a good wage, London tried never to turn him away.

Glen Ellen also was the meeting ground for some of the most famous men of San Francisco's Bohemia. London was the great star of a distinguished literary set that included such other famous characters as Ambrose Bierce, George Sterling and Joaquin Miller. London actually hated Bierce, though it was Bierce who spanned both London at the end of the nineteenth century and Mark Twain's reign over San Francisco letters some years before. It is probably not just coincidence that both Twain and especially London were instrumental in introducing the notion of realism to the then all-too-genteel world of letters. London's influence on later twentieth-century writers as diverse as Hemingway and Kerouac was pronounced.

Just before my most recent visit with Gary, I re-read Irving Stone's famed biography of London, *Sailor on Horseback.* Stone appropriated the title from an autobiography London never got around to writing. I was looking for evidence that London had indeed slept at London House. I thought I had found it when Stone mentioned that in 1906 London came to L.A. to buy livestock and stayed in the home of a sculptor friend named Felix Piano. I remembered vaguely something Gary had said, that the man who owned London House was a sculptor friend of London's. London had lived in Piano's house in Oakland as well—the Piano house there was said to be adorned with a profusion of bas-reliefs of satyrs and nymphs, as well as nudes on pedestals. Surely, I figured, Stone was talking about London House on La Vista Court in Hollywood.

Yet I wasn't so sure when I went back into old issues of the Los Angeles *Herald Examiner,* which had interviewed London during his 1906 trip. For one thing, my dream that Jack London sat on the roof of London House and saw no houses all the way to the original pueblo just could not have been true. By 1906—it was apparent from the pages of the old *Examiner*—there were more than a quarter of a million people surrounding the old pueblo.

So the first thing I asked Gary was—and I assumed his answer would be yes—were the bas-reliefs and the house built by London's friend from Oakland, Felix Piano? Gary laughed. No, he said. He had thought that, too. But the fact was, the house had been built by Finn Haakon Frolich, a sculptor and sailor friend of London's who was, as a matter of fact, a much closer friend than Piano had ever been.

I looked around the place and suddenly realized why it felt so much as though Jack London had been here. The narrow steps, the cabin-like bedroom, everything about the place gave one the feeling of being inside a ship. It was a subtle thing, but that was what Frolich had done with London House. In *Sailor on Horseback,* Stone describes Frolich as London's "court jester and sculptor" at Glen Ellen. It is Frolich's bust of London, for instance, which adorns the entrance to Glen Ellen, which today has been made into a state park and the Jack London Museum. And it is Frolich's bust of London that was cast in bronze by the Oakland Port Authority when it built Jack London Square.

Frolich was very much a part of the San Francisco Bohemia of which London was the star—and he was very much an intimate of London's. Frolich had a tremendous, booming laugh and loud voice, by all accounts. And he had been one of London's friends who witnessed the final disintegration of London during his last days at Glen Ellen.

London committed suicide in 1916 at the age of forty. In some haunting words, Frolich described the change in his friend. "He didn't do the sporting things he used to do—wrestle, play, didn't want to go into the mountains riding horseback any more. The gleam was gone from his eyes." Of course in the forty years of his life, London lived more lives than a hundred mortals combined. Interestingly enough, London predicted his own suicide in *Martin Eden,* written at the height of his career several years earlier. He said that *Martin Eden* had been written to show the folly of extreme individualism—but if London was anything, he was a great individualist as much as he was ever a socialist.

How about the inscription on the wall I had seen from George Sterling? Gary pointed to the wall—the inscription is still there. But it wasn't carved into the wall, as I had remembered; it was a decal, dark and opaque and hard to read except under a very strong light. The words were woven into a latticework of the nymphs and satyrs London's Bohemian friends all seemed to cherish. Gary said the decal had originally been sandwiched between two pieces of glass in an old sash window in the back bedroom. "The window was so rotted out I had to replace it," he explained. "Here's what it says," he added, swinging open the top part of the large barn door on the front of the London House to catch the sunlight. "'The young in heart shall find their love and laughter anywhere.' The words around the bottom of the decal are harder to make out. 'He only in Bohemia dwells who knows not he is there,'" Gary read, and paused. "There's more in the middle," he added. "'Dedicated to Finn Frolich by George Sterling.'" He paused again. "And there's a date," he slowly added. "It is 1924."

I asked Gary to repeat the date of the inscription. If Sterling inscribed the decal to his friend Frolich in 1924, and Frolich was one of the regulars at Glen Ellen during the last year of London's life, the sculptor probably didn't come to Los Angeles and build what after all was really his studio until after London's death. To my direct question—had Jack London ever slept in London House?—Gary was a bit evasive. He said that this was what had been rumored. "We found a basement downstairs, six feet square. Probably a wine cellar. We found a few things." Gary showed me a rusted metal toy locomotive. "We found this and some paper matchboxes from the '20s and some handmade bottles down there," he said. "A friend of mine suggested we keep digging because we'd probably run across some bottles London himself drank out of." But Gary said he wasn't even sure when the house was built—he estimated sometime between 1900 and 1920, "although it looks a lot older than that, I know." Gary said he was sure London House had been the only structure in the neighborhood when it was built.

Gary suggested I contact Frolich's son and daughter, one of whom he believed lived in Hollywood and the other in San Francisco. Whatever the connection of London House and Jack London, he added, he definitely knew the house was rich in Hollywood lore. Gary ought to know—he works as a script supervisor on films and television serials. La Vista Court, he said, used to be called McDougall's Lane, and McDougall's Lane sloped into a pond. Most of the scenes where a car runs into a pond in the Keystone Kops movies were shot in the alley, he said. The rest of the Keystone Kops pictures were usually shot on nearby Larchmont, which runs only a few blocks between Melrose and Third Street, Gary said.

"I've heard both Tony Quinn and John Carradine lived here. I know my friend Dick Beymer, who was a big star for some years—he was in *West Side Story*—lived here. And my friend Victor Buono almost always stays here whenever he's in town working on a movie," Gary added.

Hefty Buono? I ask. How does he get up the steep, narrow stairs? "With difficulty," Gary replies. "He always says gravity is his enemy." Gary goes on: "You know, Jack London was really one of the first writers for movies—his *Sea Wolf* was one of the first silent films. It was remade as a talking picture later with Edward G. Robinson, but Hobart Bosworth, the famed silent-screen star, played in the original *Sea Wolf*. I have a picture taken here in the house, of Frolich and Bosworth admiring Frolich's bust of Bosworth."

Gary bought the house from Frank Lopez, a pioneer Chicano activist who has since passed away. "Everyone who has had the house was somehow on a line from Jack London. Lopez was a friend of Frolich in part because of their politics. Frank was an incredible landlord. Never pried into your business or raised his rents. I became very attached to the place, so when he wanted to sell the house in 1957, I purchased it from Frank." Because London House is named after a man who had a reputation as a flaming socialist, Gary keeps his rents low, and refuses to engage in real estate speculation. That would mean tearing down the house and building apartments or breaking up old houses into bootleg apartments as Gary says some of his neighbors have done.

Virginia Forstad, Frolich's daughter, lives today in Hollywood, an old woman surrounded by mementos of the past, including pictures autographed for her by Jack London. She's not too clear about early details of her life, although she insists that she lived with her father and Jack London in the La Vista Court house. Virginia Forstad, however, is not always entirely consistent.

Her half-brother in San Francisco, Gilbert Frolich, says that his sister is a little confused, and that she lived with London and Frolich all right, but it was at the Glen Ellen ranch in Northern California. There's a famous picture of London and Virginia, who is four years of age, and Gilbert, at one-and-a-half years. The kids are nude and not in entirely respectful postures in the presence of the great author, who is wearing a black bathing suit, typical of the day, with a fishing pole in one hand and the other arm over his wife Charmian.

Unlike his half-sister, Gilbert is very precise in his recollections. Since his father's life was so mixed up with California's early Bohemian and literary history, he's made a hobby of researching his father's life. Gilbert says his father brought his children to Los Angeles from Northern California in 1920 in a Model T. He remembers that the trip, for one reason or another, took three months. Shortly after he arrived here, Frolich purchased the land on McDougall's Alley and began building his house and studio there. Although Gilbert says he realizes that Frolich's studio was widely known as London House, "he dedicated it more to himself than to Jack London." He says the bas-relief of London wasn't even finished until the middle of the Depression.

So Gilbert rules out the possibility that London ever slept at London House, even though Gary used to get mail delivered to "London House, La Vista Court, Hollywood" for many years. The post office, however, no longer will deliver mail without an address. Gilbert does offer a consolation prize over the disappointing news that London didn't sleep at London House. He said he's pretty sure George Sterling slept there.

Gilbert remembers Sterling sitting crying on the porch of some friends, not too far away from his father's sculpture studio. Gilbert went inside the house and there were his father, some friends and, of course, Sterling outside on the porch. Sterling, the elder Frolich told his son, had lost at poker and because he was a very sentimental guy he was crying. In some ways, says Gilbert, Sterling was a greater man than London. Or at least a greater character if not a writer. London wrote about Sterling as Brissenden in *Martin Eden*.

Gilbert adds that he's not sure if Anthony Quinn lived at Frolich's studio, but he's sure John Carradine did. "Mom and I came down from Oakland to put Carradine out for not paying the rent in the middle of the Depression." Carradine called the cops on Gilbert and his mother, Gilbert explains, because they were keeping a bust Carradine had made of Cecil B. DeMille. Carradine had been a sculpting student of Frolich's, and a good one at that, says Gilbert. Carradine wanted the bust because because he said he was going to "break into Hollywood" with it. Gilbert said that his mother finally relented and returned the bust to Carradine, who later did indeed present it to DeMille.

"My mother said Carradine was such a good actor that he was almost, but not quite, the only tenant ever to talk her out of collecting the rent," Gilbert says.

There's another story Gilbert insists on telling— about the red ship's lantern on the front of the house. In the mid-1930s, Finn Frolich very much liked to play the grandee, and throw great Hollywood parties. Down the street lived an old vaudeville actress, who was hurt that she hadn't been invited to a party where her kind were gathering. So she called the police. She told them that she judged, by the red lantern and the sight of happy revelers leaning out of the great barn door upstairs, that the house down the street was a whorehouse. As the cops came up the narrow steps to investigate her report, Frolich and a friend happened to be playing, on two separate pianos, but in unison, "Onward Christian Soldiers."

The cops, says Gilbert, had grins from ear to ear. They suggested that Frolich file slander charges against the actress. He did—and the vaudeville actress came to court on crutches, at which the presiding judge remarked, "Oh come on now," and adjourned everyone to his chambers to work it out. Finally everyone agreed to drop their charges and countercharges and everyone eventually became the greatest of friends. Gilbert even wound up taking out the actress's daughter—"God, she was beautiful," he says.

Gilbert says he's been writing a detailed history of the house to send to Bob Gary soon, but a couple of heart attacks have slowed him down.

Gary has nightmares when he thinks of London House being destroyed. Because the house is now in such terrible condition, he's been having lots of them recently. But the most vivid nightmare he ever had was before Jerry Brown was elected governor of California. Brown eliminated the proposed Beverly Hills Freeway, which would have demolished London House. "My nightmares used to go like this: I look out the barn door windows and I can see that the bulldozer has knocked all the other houses on La Vista Court down, and now it's making a U-turn at the end and is headed at London House," Gary said with a shudder.

But Gary has also been trying to turn his troubles with London House to the good. He's been working on a screenplay about a young writer who moves into the London House. One day the writer's girlfriend asks him if he's ever read Jack London. The young writer says no. But he begins to read London, and that changes his life and his writing—an effect which London had on many people. Gary sees the movie as a chance to do a London biography as both a documentary and a piece of fiction. Gary, who casually mentions that he's distantly related to Mark Twain, says of London: "He was the first writer who wrote about life in the raw and didn't try to sweeten it up with sugar."

Gary says that even though he's broke, he still dedicated to saving London House, although he's not sure a historical society would be interested in helping him. "I'm so angry I might just turn London House into the Church of Jack London. People will be ordained. The Bible will be Irving Stone's *Sailor on Horseback,* and we'll argue about different things London wrote. I'll take a vow of poverty and give my house, car and income to the church in exchange for it supporting me. Just the way the Catholic Church does. I won't have to pay taxes that way. If I have to do that to restore London House, I will."

We talk some more. He discusses some of the things that have been broken or stolen from the front of the house when he brings up the matter of the sign that had first attracted me to the house. Frankly, I had forgotten about the sign. Before I can ask Gary how that sign came to be affixed to London's bas-relief, he is explaining it.

"In London, England, you know, all the houses where famous writers lived have little enamel plaques. Well, a friend of mine made one of those to go under the bas-relief in front. It was just like the ones I've seen in London. It was enamel blue with white letters. It was really authentic looking."

"What did it say?" I ask, getting excited again.

"Oh my friend just made it up, I think. It said, 'Jack London slept here.'"

SEVEN

The Lost L.A. Years of Robinson Jeffers

Then what is the answer? — Not to be deluded by dreams.
To know that great civilizations have broken down into violence, and their tyrants come, many times before.
When open violence appears, to avoid it with honor or choose the least ugly faction; these evils are essential.
To keep one's own integrity, be merciful and uncorrupted and not wish for evil; and not be duped
By dreams of universal justice or happiness. These dreams will not be fulfilled.
To know this, and know that however ugly the parts appear the whole remains beautiful. A severed hand
Is an ugly thing, and man disseuered from the earth and stars and his history . . . for contemplation or in fact . . .
Often appears atrociously ugly. Integrity is wholeness, the greatest beauty is
Organic wholeness, the wholeness of life and things, the divine beauty of the universe. Love that, not man
Apart from that, or else you will share man's pitiful confusions, or drown in despair when his days darken.

[ROBINSON JEFFERS]

The other day I ran into John Harris, proprietor of Papa Bach Bookstore, the distinguished West Los Angeles emporium of the printed word. Harris is also a poet and a publisher, the closest thing Los Angeles has to a literary Renaissance man.

I respect Harris, and I listened when he mused aloud: "I don't know why no one has ever written about Robinson Jeffers as an L.A. boy. He spent his formative years here. He's a very important and great poet, the last of the great narrative poets. The tradition of narra-

tive poetry, which is all but dead now, went back to the Greeks, and Jeffers was the last in the tradition. I also never understood why his poems weren't made into movies; they seemed such naturals."

Jeffers is best known for his association with the Big Sur coast. He and his wife, Una, moved to Carmel in 1914, but his poetry was so strongly linked with Big Sur it seemed as if he had always been there. In fact, most of the Jeffers scholars who sift through the poet's early work looking for clues to the mature work written in Carmel, do so in Los Angeles.

In an effort to trace the characters in Jeffers' poems geographically, Harris actually went to Big Sur and also wrote letters to everyone who might have known Jeffers. Harris gave me a packet of his research – including a letter to Harris from the astronomer Hamilton Jeffers, the poet's brother. There was an essay by Harris called "Testaments and Revelations: A Study of Robinson Jeffers as an Historian," which pointed out again Jeffers' link to Southern California. "The years before Carmel," Harris wrote, "had seen Jeffers devote his wide-ranging interests to the study of such subjects as literature, religion, philosophy, languages, geology, medicine, forestry, zoology and the law."

Harris makes the point even more strongly. "It wasn't only his academic studies, which were prodigious at both Occidental and USC. He acquired his love of nature in the nearby San Gabriel Mountains, and he first fell in love with the Pacific not at Carmel but in Hermosa and Manhattan beaches."

I discovered Jeffers' poetry in the mid-1960s when the Sierra Club and Ballantine Books issued *Not Man Apart,* which included photographs of the Big Sur coast, matched – in a sometimes fragmentary way – with poems from Jeffers. A lot of my old buddies and I were in the habit then of leaving L.A. in the morning and sleeping on a Big Sur beach that evening. There was no better way to escape the city – which so many of us seemed to want to do – than by walking down through the fog and mist of a wet, green Big Sur can-

yon in the dark to a moonlit beach, where we'd sleep overnight. Then we'd awaken the next morning, letting the sense of the place bathe us with something very eternal. Jeffers captures that eternal something in far less prosaic words than my own.

The first time I opened *Not Man Apart,* it was in anticipation of seeing Edward Weston's famed photographs. But it was Jeffers' poetry that sidetracked me. I do not think I had ever read words so powerful, so full of a sense of the apocalypse mixed with such a strong sense of the cosmos.

I heard of Jeffers again when I was a writer-in-residence in 1971 at Villa Montalvo, a copy of an Italian villa built in the coastal mountains close to Santa Cruz and Monterey, not so very far from Big Sur. Montalvo is now run as a center for the arts and an arboretum by Santa Clara County and a group of art patrons. But it was built in the 1920s by James Phelan, the U.S. Senator from California and colorful bachelor mayor of San Francisco. Phelan apparently had a penchant for fancy women as well as the finest in the fine arts. So the legend of Villa Montalvo that I learned about while I was there was that Phelan used to stage both poetry readings and orgies there – the place seems a likely site for both or either. Legend also has it that Jeffers was the star of these affairs, although Jeffers scholars in L.A. have assured me it is unlikely that Una or Jeffers would have partaken of the joys of orgies – even if the pair of them had left L.A. under a cloud of public scandal.

I knew of Jeffers only as a great poet connected with Northern California. Yet it was from Southern California that Jeffers and Una emigrated when he began building their granite "Tor House" in Big Sur in 1914. Jeffers was then twenty-seven. During the previous decade, he had been developing and maturing as a young man in Los Angeles, but it was in his stone tower "on the continent's edge" that he found his voice.

By the time Jeffers' career began to flourish in the

1920s, people had forgotten that he had grown up in Los Angeles, so identified with Carmel and Big Sur had his work become. Perhaps Los Angeles never properly celebrated Jeffers as one of its own because Jeffers' career declined so precipitously in the 1950s, just when Los Angeles was beginning to grow up and collect its own legends.

In fact, Jeffers had achieved, if not a great literary reputation, certainly some notoriety in Los Angeles before his move to Big Sur.

Jeffers burst onto the world poetry scene as the author of epic narrative poems, full of melodrama, storm and fury. They were modern-day Greek dramas—his themes were sexual and brutal. They dealt with things like fratricide, adultery, incest and bestiality. His greatest epic poems were novels in poetry, shocking works like "Roan Stallion," "Tamar," "Give Your Heart to the Hawks," "Thurso's Landing," and "Cawdor." Jeffers' characters followed their tragic and inevitable paths to doom against a beautiful but totally inhuman backdrop of primeval nature in the form of Jeffers' Big Sur landscape. This backdrop was Jeffers' reality and his cosmic view, and it was the most distinctive quality of his poems.

His works were still selling well in the 1930s, but his increasingly anti-Roosevelt stance was not helping him in terms of public opinion. He was culturally, as well as politically, a very conservative and traditional man. He was a staunch Republican, which was an unusual stance for a poet.

It was Jeffers' political isolationism in the 1940s that really finished him off as far as the general public was concerned. But for the efforts of a few Jeffers fanatics, he might have been forgotten in the 1950s, although he was still appreciated in Europe. It was not until a few years after his death in 1962 that his reputation again began to grow. Undoubtedly, the *Not Man Apart* volume had a lot to do with this.

I walked out of John Harris's bookstore armed not only with Harris's personal files on Jeffers, but also carrying some rare, prized editions by and about Jeffers from Harris's own collection.

I next sought out Robert J. Brophy, professor of English at California State University at Long Beach, because he had not only written a highly respected volume on Jeffers—*Robinson Jeffers: Myth, Ritual and Symbol in His Narrative Poems*—but he is also the editor of the Robinson Jeffers Newsletter. Brophy and his gang of Jeffers fanatics have spent long hours retracing Jeffers' life in Los Angeles. "We're always looking for letters, pictures, old buildings and so on relating to Jeffers," Brophy says.

When talking about Jeffers' Los Angeles period, Brophy observes: "A Freudian analyst would be delighted with the material of Jeffers' early life. I mean, Jeffers' dad was a very strange bird, twice the age of Jeffers' mother, who had lacked a strong father image in her childhood. Jeffers' father was very stern and strict. Jeffers' mother turned her emotional life onto her son. And there was a lifelong antagonism between father and son."

Brophy says that his father forced Jeffers to study such a prodigious amount of Latin and Greek and other classical subjects that the boy developed headaches. The young Jeffers was finally sent away from his native Pennsylvania to private schools mostly in and around Zurich. Even in the Alps, Jeffers was not safe from his father, who would show up every six months or so and move his son to another school. Consequently, Robinson Jeffers became very shy and did not learn how to make friends.

In Los Angeles, however, Jeffers "seems to have gone through a freeing period. He seems to have made an amicable break with his father, to have lived a lot on his own. He had lots of love affairs, did lots of drinking, things his father would not have approved of. It was a real maturing period for his intellect," Brophy declares.

Jeffers' father was a minister, a distinguished professor emeritus at a Presbyterian seminary, intellectually a rather liberal man for his day, but personally a combination of eccentricity and strictness. In the small suburb of Pittsburgh where Jeffers spent his childhood, he never had a chance to make friends. This was because whenever he'd start to get friendly with anybody, his father would react by moving the entire family to the outskirts of town, where there was nobody. The elder Jeffers wanted his son to study, and he told his wife to take careful note of Robinson's development because one day the information would be needed by biographers.

One day in 1903 the minister retrieved his son from Switzerland and moved his whole brood to California, where he kept up his curious habit of restlessly moving from place to place. The first house the Jefferses had in the Southland was a cottage in Long Beach – no one remembers where exactly. Soon, however, the good doctor found a lot in Highland Park, and in 1904 he spent four thousand dollars to have a two-story frame house built. The house still stands at 346 W. Avenue 57. The elder Jeffers moved his family to Highland Park so Robinson could attend nearby Occidental College, then a small Presbyterian college with a student body of some two hundred souls.

Jeffers, just entering his young manhood in Los Angeles, began to shed some of his shyness at Occidental. He became the editor of the literary magazine in which he published many of his early poems, mostly about the joys of exploring the San Gabriel Mountains. Occidental College still maintains an extensive collection in its Robinson Jeffers Room, and the college librarian, Tyrus G. Harmsen, is a Jeffers authority of no inconsiderable note.

Jeffers' infatuation with nature was legendary among his Occidental classmates. Those who went hiking with him say his vitality was simply incredible; he walked with a magnificent stride few could equal, reciting verse from Tennyson and Homer. When it was time to make camp, Jeffers was always willing to pitch in and do more than his share. He simply never

tired. And during the days on the trail, he didn't mind carrying more than his share on his back.

Not long after the Occidental period, Jeffers became familiar with and began to love the ocean as well as the mountains of the Los Angeles area. Jeffers' father was getting restless again, and so in 1905, when Robinson, at the age of eighteen, graduated with honors, the Highland Park home was sold. The Jefferses first moved to a house a block south from the shore on Third Street in Manhattan Beach, but then moved a mile back from the water to an eighty-acre ranch in the vicinity of what is now Sepulveda and Manhattan Beach Boulevards. It was on these South Bay beaches that Jeffers first came to love the Pacific and to call it "the one ocean." Neither of his Manhattan Beach places exist today.

Jeffers spent the summer with his family in Manhattan Beach and then decided to enter the University of Southern California for his master's degree in letters. He met Una in a German class at USC. When he met her in 1906, however, Una was married to another man, a prominent Los Angeles attorney named Ted Kuster.

Brophy's *Robinson Jeffers Newsletter* has published, from time to time, information on Una, the bored socialite wife of Ted Kuster. She was more than once on the society pages because she was, among other things, the Southland's premier woman automobile racer. Brophy, who has recently been reading letters just discovered about Una in those early days, says she was not altogether an appealing creature. She was very pretty, and very demanding. Her husband, who doted on her, supplied her with her own seamstress – for she insisted on having only the most exquisite clothes. "She was very manipulative," says Brophy, "and used her sexuality on everybody. She was very proud and very vain. Later, of course, as the wife of Robinson Jeffers of Carmel, she led a very austere life in Tor House. It's amazing how she changed later in life."

It was not necessarily love at first sight between the somewhat dilettante Mrs. Kuster and Robinson when they met on the USC campus in 1906. In fact, it wasn't until 1909 – and quite likely later – that their romance became physical and passionate. Early on, when curiousity got the better of Una's friends and they asked who the young man was who always accompanied her, she is supposed to have replied,"He's a very gifted linguist and writes very immature poetry."

Immature or not, there is a hint of the antipathy Jeffers was to develop in his later poem,"The City," in a poem he published in 1906 in the USC *Courier.* The poem describes a particular hill he often went to, to look out on the city. He describes sitting there, looking down on the streets full of traffic, and the traffic raising its "multitudinous voice" in a roar over a city hidden by gray and black smoke. The young poet declared he liked the whole place better at night."It is lovelier, with its bareness hidden out of sight, all gemmed with wondrous fairy lights." On the perimeter of the poet's view danced "furnace fire lights" whose "rolling fierce shafts" pierced the black skies.

In 1907 Jeffers' parents decided to move to Europe. Robinson followed for a short while, with the intention of entering the University of Zürich. But he felt constrained by constant parental supervision, so he left his family in Europe and returned alone to Los Angeles. He re-enrolled at USC, this time in the medical school. He was living in a row house that still stands at 1623 Shatto Street, near downtown Los Angeles. He also began spending more and more time with the pretty Mrs. Kuster, and the gossip began to sizzle.

In the summer months, the Kusters lived in a house on Hermosa Beach. Jeffers rented a room with a Mrs. Melinda Nash, not too far away. While Kuster worked, Jeffers and Una, and sometimes other friends of hers, dallied on the beach. By this time things had gone quite far. Even though they saw each other every day, they exchanged daily love letters. During this period,

Jeffers wrote his "At Playa Hermosa," in which he describes having neither "despair nor hope" as he watched the "gray waves rise and drop." It ends with these strangely prophetic words: "Strange and ominous peace abides. What will Fate exact of me/For this quiet by the sea?"

Once, on a hike to Mount Lowe in the San Gabriel Mountains, Mrs. Ted Kuster proposed marriage to Jeffers during a romantic interlude replete with a detective the lady's unfortunate husband had hired. During this period too, wrote Lawrence Clark Powell, "his love of poetry and nature deepened. He had a passion for birds, winds, sunsets, long solitary walks, and would go alone on trips, afoot or on horseback, into the mountains." If he wasn't in the mountains, said Powell, he was at the beach, meaning Redondo or Hermosa. "On that blue Pacific bay he roamed the wharves and hobnobbed with longshoremen unloading fragrant Oregon pine from coasting schooners, or drank with them at night in waterfront saloons."

Of course the romance with Una was still the most important thing that happened to him in Los Angeles.

Although he had returned alone to Southern California, his parents had followed not too far behind. They settled again in Los Angeles, and soon were off to Seattle. Jeffers took the opportunity to go away with them in 1910 and get away from Una. He thought he would study forestry in the Northwest. He didn't stay long, though. Una and Jeffers had said they must never see each other again. Within a half hour of Jeffers' return from the Northwest, he saw Una at a crosswalk. She was sitting in a large open roadster right there in front of him. They tried to avoid each other's eyes, but realized it was impossible. They were hopelessly in love.

In the meantime, the elder Jefferses had tired of the Northwest and moved back to Los Angeles, where they purchased a house that still stands at 822 Garfield Avenue in Pasadena. It was at this time that Jeffers published his first book of poetry. It was printed by a Los Angeles print shop in 1912 at Jeffers' expense. The book was called *Flagons and Apples* and was well received by at least one Los Angeles newspaper, whose reviewer asked Jeffers to write the review of the book under the reviewer's name. The reviewer thought quite highly of Jeffers, obviously.

One gets more insight into Jeffers' life during this time from his own description of the period in 1912 just before *Flagons and Apples* was published. The reminiscence was one of the few pieces of prose Jeffers ever published. It appeared in 1932 in a fine-printing magazine called *The Colphonio,* which came from the presses of Ward Ritchie.

This was in Los Angeles and I lived rather solitarily at one of the beaches [Hermosa] twenty miles distant, and was too young for my age, and drank a good deal when I came to town. At Redondo, on my way home in the evening, I left the electric car to visit a barroom frequented by longshoremen friends of mine. I stayed there until the cars stopped running and had to walk the three miles home. For several hours I had thought nothing about my verse, which only interested part of my mind, for I had no confidence in them. It was not until the next morning that I looked for the bundle of manuscripts which had been under my arm, but it must have been laid down somewhere . . . either at home or in Redondo.

Luckily, Jeffers goes on to explain, he knew his own verse by heart, and was able to retype a new draft for the printers.

One of Brophy's friends and fellow researchers for the Robinson Jeffers Newsletter is Robert Kafka. He is a self-described Jeffers fanatic who has retraced much of Jeffers' life in Los Angeles, doing even such tedious jobs as researching county court records. Kafka knows, for instance, by first-hand research, the various bars Jeffers went drinking in, and has even uncovered the fact that Jeffers was involved in—though

did not cause—a bloody barroom brawl in a place called The Ship's Cafe, which was built in the shape of a ship on the old Venice pier. Kafka says Jeffers also used to haunt a number of bars, now all gone, on South Spring Street in a downtown area that's now "all modern banks and parking lots."

Neither Brophy nor his friend Kafka have been able to uncover exactly where Mrs. Nash's house was in Hermosa Beach, which is where Jeffers stayed when he wanted to get away from the city, and also see Una, which was often. A close relationship between the young Jeffers and Mrs. Nash quickly developed. Jeffers described her as his adopted mother. She kept his apartment on the second floor always ready for him, and she looked after him when he was there. Young Jeffers was by no means a perfect tenant. One time he went away and, by oversight, left his dog locked in the bedroom. The dog tore up all the furniture.

Brophy's newsletter tracked down a John DeWitt of Costa Mesa who knew both Jeffers and Mrs. Nash. DeWitt said Mrs. Nash's place was "a big brown house on the crest of the hill in Hermosa, overlooking the Pacific to the west, and the Japanese vegetable gardens to the east." DeWitt told the newsletter that Jeffers used to take him walking, and "would read some of his poems to me, which at my tender age were not fully comprehended."

Mrs. Nash, says DeWitt, was a seamstress from Wisconsin, an old and valued employee of the DeWitt family there. Mrs. Nash was apparently quite good at what she did and had made some money. She retired to Hermosa Beach, and later invited the DeWitts to stay with her when they moved out to L.A. DeWitt said that Mrs. Nash had transferred her love from a dead grandson to Jeffers, who "was a temperamental, introspective and reclusive young man. He would be closeted in his room for hours, writing, completely oblivious to regular mealtimes. He would often go downstairs in the middle of the night and Mrs. Nash would get up and prepare a meal for him."

The tragedy of Mrs. Nash was that she was a strict Victorian. At one point late in the game Jeffers and Una, not exactly a chaste bride, asked Mrs. Nash along on a trip they wanted to take to Seattle. Mrs. Nash was to be the chaperone—a role that Mrs. Nash believed in very strongly. Such were the times. But in this case she was so shocked at the impropriety of the thing that she refused Jeffers' request. Robinson and Una went to Seattle, as history now knows, anyway. Mrs. Nash became quite depressed—DeWitt said he found out why when the headlines broke on Friday morning, February 28, 1913. One scandal-loving morning sheet, which still publishes in downtown L.A., ran the story under the headline, "Love's Gentle Alchemy To Weld Broken Lives." It was the same newspaper that used to carry on and on about Mrs. Una Kuster's car-racing days on its society pages. But this time, a society matron had suddenly jumped onto the news pages. What the Friday morning edition told was the tale of prominent attorney Ed Kuster divorcing his wife Una; Kuster intended to take a plump lass from Bakersfield as his second wife.

Ah, delicious scandal! The story explained to the breathless denizens of L.A. that the divorce proceedings of the socially prominent couple had been "shrouded by a veil of mystery." But the newspaper had talked to people in the know, and it could authoritatively report that behind the Kuster divorce was the stalking, "unseen but potent figure of the inevitable triangle." The "potent figure" was a member of a mystic cult which "professes to believe that those things which conscience permits are right." Jeffers was named as the "potent figure."

The next day the same newspaper was still carrying on about the affair. "Two Points of the Eternal Triangle," the headline blared. There was a box with pictures of Una and Jeffers, and his poem, "On the Cliff," which was a love poem from *Flagons and Apples,* under the right side of the headline. On the left was a single-column deck head: "Parents Wash Hands of It." The point of this story was to report that Mrs. J.H. Jeffers, "mother of John Robinson Jeffers, the lyric expounder of melancholy poems of passion," wasn't going to comment on her son's affair, that his destiny was his own.

The newspaper went on to proclaim that Mrs. Kuster had, in reality, been "made the scapegoat of a coterie of faddists who egged her on. In the beginning," said the story, "Mrs. Kuster was used by these individualists," who are unnamed in the article, "to ascertain just how far society, or that portion of society they represent, would go in accepting the new thought wherein the 'I' becomes the absolute, and once conscience is muffled, all is right." Intriguing stuff? It seems also that poor Mrs. Kuster was "sincere in her actions, whatever they were," according to the newspaper. "When upon one occasion an attempt was made to induce her to experiment with another candidate for superman distinction, she turned from the proposition in abhorrence."

The story quite shocked Mrs. Nash and no doubt confirmed her worst fears. Still, after Jeffers and Una had run off to Seattle and finally had gotten married in Tacoma, Jeffers wrote Mrs. Nash an affectionate letter. He said that the newly married pair—himself and his bride, Una—planned to return to "L.A.—and Hermosa"—but only for three weeks, before they departed for Europe. Jeffers signed the letter, "Goodnight, my dear Nash, Robin."

Una and Jeffers returned to the Southland, but didn't make it to Europe until some years later. Happy as lovebirds, the poet and his wife stayed with the senior Jefferses in Pasadena. It was soon apparent that she was pregnant, however, so it was decided that they would stay in the Southland and take advantage of American medicine. They rented a place in La Jolla, where they stayed a number of months. They didn't return to Los Angeles until a month before Una had a baby girl on May 5, 1914, at the Good Samaritan Hospital. They named the baby Maeve, but she lived only five days.

When the Jefferses first moved to La Jolla, Kuster and his new bride followed suit. The four of them used to go walking in the hills and along the beach in La Jolla, and no doubt that included nearby Torrey Pines. "Everything was so weird," says Brophy, "but Jeffers always allowed things just to happen. His attitude seemed to be that that was the price of life, that's just how things were." Kuster later became a neighbor of the Jefferses in Carmel.

The Jefferses realized, soon after their first child's death, that they would have to find someplace other than Europe to settle, for the war was now very much on. Jeffers had been quite fond of La Jolla, however. During the months in La Jolla, he was becoming more and more attached to the sea, and less and less anxious to live in a city, where people piled in on top of each other. Jeffers wrote an old Occidental classmate, Dan S. Hammack Jr., a Los Angeles lawyer, that he knew of no "Southern Californian beach more beautiful" than La Jolla. He mentioned that despite La Jolla's increasing amount of civilization, there were still abalone, seals, porpoises and pelicans around. Nonetheless, they were not considering it for a permanent home.

The Jefferses first heard of Carmel, the oasis in the north, from one of Una's old friends, the poet Frederick Mortimer Clapp. From the moment Jeffers and Una laid eyes on the Big Sur coast, they knew they had found what they were looking for. "For the first time in my life," Jeffers would later say, "I could see people living—amid magnificently unspoiled scenery—essentially as they did in the Idylls or the Sagas, or in Homer's Ithaca. . . . Men were riding after cattle, or plowing the headland, hovered over by white sea gulls, as they had done for thousands of years, and will for thousands of years to come. Here was contemporary life that was also permanent life."

As is now clear from his poetry, Jeffers found his voice in the granite house he built himself on the Big Sur coast. His restlessness and need to move from place to place, obviously brought on by his father, disappeared. Yet in looking back on his life, Jeffers himself noted some of the formative elements in his mature work, and they were all things that occurred in turn-of-the-century Los Angeles.

For example, at nineteen years of age he came across the quote from the German philosopher Friedrich Nietzsche: "The poets lie too much." Jeffers decided he agreed with that and worked on making himself the exception that proves the rule. He became a very uncompromising kind of poet, who wrote only about things he thought would last, would be eternal.

And it was also in Los Angeles that Jeffers met Una, of course. Their intellectual relationship was a major component of their love. Jeffers credited her as the co-author of everything good that he went on to write, even though "she never saw the poem until I had finished it." Often it was Una who would go out and listen to the gossip, the legends, which Jeffers weaved so powerfully into his narrative poems of Big Sur.

She was the sociable half of the couple; he liked only good friends, like George Sterling, the unofficial California poet laureate who was a Carmel native. (This was the same George Sterling who had been Jack London's friend.) Once Una actually got her husband to agree to go to a party of literati in Carmel. He faked a faint after a few minutes and they had to go home.

While Los Angeles was important in Jeffers' development, Carmel was his nirvana. He and Una chose that as their identity completely. While Jeffers didn't write anything saying how he summed up Los Angeles, he did mention how much Una hated the Southland. Jeffers himself encouraged people to think of the Jeffers before Carmel as a different person than the Jeffers of Carmel. To one fellow who later complained that he wished he had known Jeffers in his Los Angeles decade, Jeffers replied that "Luckily perhaps . . . we didn't meet in 1911. I remember humbly a rather queer young person called by my name then."

Una and Jeffers seemed profoundly to change each other, just as Big Sur profoundly changed them both. He wrote his best poetry there, and in the 1920s had a considerable popular following. His books went through many printings, even though he didn't do the things successful poets are supposed to do, like go on the poetry-reading circuit. Jeffers was a hermit. He didn't like groups of people. He was an oddity, hard to categorize in many ways.

The Jeffers of Carmel was a staunch Republican, very conservative in politics as well as philosophy. Yet the critic who put him on the map as a poet, after California writers George Sterling and Lawrence Clark Powell had written early books about him, was the editor of the then-influential communist magazine in New York, *New Masses*. James Rorty not only wrote about Jeffers, but used all his influence to get others to do so as well. The irony of a Marxist literary czar promoting a poet with politics only slightly to the left of Atilla the Hun was not lost on Rorty himself, who said, "I think Jeffers is one of the best poets alive. I don't share his philosophy. What of it? He writes with greater poetic intensity than any other living poet I have read." Today Jeffers' poetry has a sizable audience behind the Iron Curtain.

I finally was able to get in touch with Lawrence Clark Powell, author of *Robinson Jeffers, The Man and His Work*, published in Los Angeles in the mid-1930s, and chief librarian at UCLA for many years. Today Powell, as Professor Emeritus at the University of Arizona, feels vindicated by his early championing of the cause of Jeffers. The last decade has seen a Jeffers renaissance, Powell proclaims. "There's been half a dozen books about him. There's a Robinson Jeffers Newsletter now coming out of Occidental College. And his books are coming back into print."

Powell denies that Jeffers was just a misanthropic visionary. "He was a very hard-nosed, intellectual realist. He wasn't embittered. He was in his daily life a very happy man who said he'd like to go on living as he did for centuries."

Powell also says he does not believe Los Angeles or the scandal involving Una embittered Jeffers. He said the great anti-city sentiments in Jeffers' later poetry were written "about no place whatsoever. It was a philosophical concept of cities. He was writing out of his mind, not his life."

Maybe so, but I've never been able to believe that the life of the mind can be separated from that of the surrounding environment, especially in Jeffers' case, where he constructed the stages for his poetic sagas out of recognizable parts of the landscape, both in Big Sur and in Los Angeles.

EIGHT

In Search of
Upton Sinclair

Despite the fact that the centennial of Upton Sinclair's birthday was celebrated a couple of summers ago at Los Angeles State College, the sad truth for Robert O. Hahn is that the greatest muck-raking author of them all has fallen on hard times in his own country—even here in Southern California, where Sinclair lived and worked and was very much a part of local history for more than half a century. Hahn is the education professor at L.A. State who publishes

Uppie Speaks, also known, for the sake of proper academicians, as the *Upton Sinclair Quarterly.* Hahn is further saddened to note that if people remember Upton Sinclair's name at all, they confuse him with his now more famous protégé, Sinclair Lewis. Yet Sinclair Lewis himself admitted that his *Elmer Gantry* was inspired by Upton Sinclair's *Profits of Religion.* Back in 1906, Sinclair Lewis had been a member of Upton Sinclair's utopian commune, Helicon Hall, just outside New York City. At that time, Sinclair Lewis was a young, unknown writer and Upton Sinclair had just become a national celebrity because of *The Jungle.*

Hahn does not necessarily disagree with those who say Sinclair Lewis wrote consistently better literature than Upton Sinclair. But if you count the thousands of letters, pamphlets and magazine articles, in addition to some seventy-eight books, Hahn says it would certainly be possible to argue that no writer ever had a greater impact than Upton Sinclair. And some of Sinclair's books were acknowledged masterpieces – books such as *Jimmie Higgins* and *The Goose-Step,* an exposé about higher education that focused on the University of Southern California.

Not only was Sinclair incredibly prolific; he was also a self-published author, operating out of post office boxes in Pasadena, Long Beach and Monrovia. He published hundreds of thousands of copies of his own books from the various Southland homes he lived in after 1915. Yet when Sinclair Lewis accepted the Nobel Prize for literature in 1930, he chastized the prize-givers for not having so honored Upton Sinclair, "of whom you must say, whether you admire or detest his aggressive socialism, that he is internationally better-known than any other American artist whosoever, be he novelist, poet, painter, sculptor, musician, architect."

Lewis was not the only person who wanted Sinclair to have the Nobel Prize. Albert Einstein, Bertrand Russell and George Bernard Shaw, among others, signed petitions to the Nobel committee. Many people were also shocked that Sinclair never received the Pulitzer Prize for *The Jungle,* the book which forced the president and Congress to pass the nation's first pure-food-and-drug laws. He was finally given the Pulitzer for *Dragon's Teeth,* one of his immensely popular Lanny Budd series, written later in his life.

Hahn is of the opinion that Sinclair's star has fallen for much the same reason Lewis mentioned in his Nobel speech. It was simply, says Hahn, that his militant socialism branded him as someone to ignore. Hahn says that even at L.A. State, "the snobs, the literati in the English Department ignore him," and that it is that way across the nation in all the country's colleges and universities now. The result, Hahn says, is that Sinclair isn't being presented to students in high schools any more, either.

Yet in Europe, Sinclair remains a popular American writer, whose work is always being reprinted. There's a brand new biography of Upton Sinclair coming out in German, Hahn says, and German television recently completed an in-depth biography which was shot in Los Angeles and in the San Gabriel Valley. "That tells you something. Television here has just ignored him."

Hahn points out that the only biography of Sinclair around now is Leon Harris's *Upton Sinclair: American Rebel,* published in 1975. Hahn adds that Harris might as well have subtitled his book "The Forgotten American Rebel," because it didn't do very well, "even though it was a pretty good book." When Hahn taught an unusual course on Upton Sinclair as part of L.A. State's American Studies program, he had trouble buying copies of Sinclair's last book, his autobiography.

But was Sinclair a great writer? I asked Hahn more than once. Hahn agrees that this is not an easy question to answer. For one thing, because his books were self-published he had to edit them himself. Most writers, including the best, need editors, Hahn points out. So Sinclair is inconsistent, but his problem is that he was different as well. His style was quite different from other styles at the turn of the century, Hahn says. "It's almost a documentary style, closer to the current journalistic style; you know, something like Truman Capote's *In Cold Blood*. The thing about Sinclair is that he had an incredible lifespan. He was a link in our history. He began writing for a living at seventeen and wrote into his eighties. It's a curious thing," says Hahn; "it's as though the socialist put-down of his time has lived with him all these years."

Hahn suspects that the L.A. State College administration rejected the idea of supporting *Uppie Speaks* because of something to do with Sinclair's politics. The administration pointed out that since the school's English department didn't take Sinclair seriously as a writer, it consequently regarded the quarterly as Hahn's personal project.

Hahn points out that the quarterly has an editorial board, that it is edited by the special collections librarian at Long Beach State University. Furthermore, Hahn says, its editorial board includes graduate students who care enough about the publication to meet and discuss it every Thursday night. It has about thirty other regular supporters, including Sinclair's former literary agent, his doctor, the late famed movie producer Sol Lesser, who was also a good friend and collaborator of Sinclair's, and novelist Irving Wallace.

Hahn was introduced to Sinclair's writings when he was growing up in the East before World War II, and once he had discovered Sinclair, he could not stop hunting for more to read. By the time he arrived in Los Angeles in 1948, he had thirty Sinclair volumes in his personal library.

Sinclair came to Coronado, on San Diego Bay, in 1915, and settled in Pasadena in 1916, a decade after *The Jungle* had made him a national celebrity. His exposé of the meat-packing industry may have hit the public's stomach and not its heart, but it had propelled him into world-class fame. Sinclair and President Theodore Roosevelt developed a rather tense but personal relationship over the book; Roosevelt was sometimes a "trust-buster," but he most certainly was no socialist. And in fact, Sinclair's writing may have made more converts to vegetarianism than to socialism. Although he himself was both a vegetarian and a socialist, his graphic descriptions of the adulteration and poisoning of meat products as well as the unsanitary conditions which were commonplace in packing houses revolted the public. Further investigations revealed that *The Jungle* was not only a gripping novel, it was devastatingly accurate reportage.

After *The Jungle*, Sinclair couldn't do anything without it showing up in the penny-dreadful New York "yellow press." By 1908 he was close to a nervous breakdown. His breakup with his first wife, Meta, had become lurid headlines everywhere he went. At the same time George Sterling, who seems to have been a friend of every important California writer of the day from Jack London to poet Robinson Jeffers, was coaxing Sinclair to come west. So was another socialist, millionaire H. Gaylord Wilshire, after whom Los Angeles's Wilshire Boulevard was named, and about whom we shall hear much more. Wilshire had a gold mine in the Sierras, whose two unusual main features were plenty of "high wages and socialist propaganda." Sinclair finally came west, and stayed both in the Sierras and in Carmel.

He was welcomed by no less a personage than his fellow muckraker, Lincoln Steffens, who wrote him in Carmel, "You are in my state, you know—California, the most beautiful lady in the union—and you are in a beautiful place in that beautiful state." At that time, Steffens wanted Sinclair to come to Sacramento and visit the Steffens household there. Sinclair didn't go to Sacramento that time but, ironically, in 1934 when Sinclair ran for and almost won the governorship, he did visit the Steffens home—for the Steffens home in Sacramento had become the governor's mansion.

Those who grew up in the Golden State during the Great Depression no doubt remember Sinclair and his "End Poverty in California" movement, the EPIC plan. It won him the Democratic nomination, and he lost to the Republicans with forty-five percent of the vote only after one of the most vicious political smear campaigns ever launched. Nonetheless, Sinclair's candidacy forced a realignment of the two major political parties, and out of the EPIC movement came such later Democratic officeholders as U.S. Senator Sheridan Downey, Governor Culbert Olson, Congressman Jerry Voorhis and Los Angeles County Supervisor John Anson Ford.

But that is jumping ahead of our tale a bit. After his first visit to California, primarily Northern California, during 1908, Sinclair was forced to return to the East. He did return to Southern California in 1915, and the reason was simple. Like everyone else, he loved the climate. "It's good for the body and it's good for the mind," he announced. By the end of his long stay here, he had decided he could not imagine ever having to live in any other part of the world.

Sinclair's first view of California had been George Sterling's writers' and artists' colony at Carmel in 1908. But when he finally found the ideal place for himself and his new wife, Mary Craig, in 1916, he chose that most unsocialist of places—Pasadena. He described Pasadena as "the city of millionaires" and he was certainly right. The nation's "plutocracy," to use Sinclair's word, had been spending their summers in Pasadena for some while—in the days before air-conditioning, they used to like to leave the muggy, hot East and spend their time in the mansions and great hotels of Pasadena. One of their favorite activities was playing tennis. As a matter of fact, one of Sinclair's favorite activities was playing tennis. He once ranked as Pasadena's seventh best tennis player.

It was certainly not out of character for Sinclair to love what was then that most plutocratic of sports, tennis. For the nation's most notorious socialist was in fact very much a genteel aristocrat. His father had been a drunk, but, like his mother, he was proud of being from Confederate Navy aristocracy. Furthermore,

through his mother's family Sinclair was related to the Blands, one of the wealthiest families in Baltimore.

The split between poor and rich was very real to Sinclair. A great part of his childhood was spent in wretched poverty in New York, but he sometimes lived in the mansions of his rich relatives in Baltimore. In *Upton Sinclair: American Rebel*, author Leon Harris suggests that it was this double exposure that had formed his character. Sinclair's life was an odd variation on the Horatio Alger theme: he had risen out of the slums to make himself a great success through his writing, but he had never aspired to riches, as did most other successful Americans who lifted themselves from poverty and slums by their own bootstraps. Instead, he wanted an explanation for the chasm he saw between the rich and the poor. Social justice, not wealth, was his obsession.

Significantly, Sinclair discovered socialism in *Wilshire's Magazine*, which was published by H. Gaylord Wilshire. He first saw the magazine in 1902 in a New York editor's office. He used to prowl editorial offices for work because he'd discovered early on that he had a knack for writing pulp magazine fiction, and while he was still a teenager he supported himself and his poor parents with his hack work.

One of the greatest moments in his life was when he finally got to meet Wilshire. Wilshire had made and lost several fortunes in L.A. real estate, but whenever he made money he always plowed it into his socialist ventures, be they magazines or mines. By 1895, Wilshire had been sure that the boulevard to which he had given his name would become the "fashionable concourse and driveway" of L.A. He was right, of course—Wilshire Boulevard was destined to become L.A.'s answer to the Champs Elysée of Paris, Fifth Avenue in New York and Michigan Avenue in Chicago.

Yet in a sense, Wilshire's great visionary powers may have affected the world more through their impact on the young mind of Upton Sinclair than through their impact on L.A. maps. After discovering Wilshire's magazine, Sinclair spent the rest of his long career pouring his socialist vision into nearly everything he wrote. It has often been pointed out, however, that Sinclair's great accomplishments were social reforms, rather than a transformation of society from capitalism to socialism. Thus such varied people as John Kennedy, Bertolt Brecht, Aleksander Solzhenitsyn, Leon Trotsky, Sergei Eisenstein, Herbert Marcuse, Ramsey Clark, Robert McNamara, Eric Sevareid, Patrick Moynihan, Norman Mailer, Maxim Gorki and Mahatma Gandhi claimed to have been deeply affected by his writings.

Although Sinclair was often called a communist, Lenin contemptuously dismissed him as "an emotional socialist." Sinclair's socialism was not generally of the Marxist variety; it was more of a utopian populism, with deep roots in the American experience. There was something almost religious about Sinclair, something very saintly about him. In appearance, he was a frail, rather ascetic-looking man. He was often described as an American Zola or Balzac, but he was puritan in his private habits. He certainly was no hedonist. He didn't drink and probably spent most of his lifetime, after his disastrous first marriage, as a celibate—at least that is what Dr. Hahn believes.

He was also a health-food nut, always experimenting with yet another miracle diet. Both he and Wilshire fell prey to a San Francisco homeopathic physician named Abrams, whose "I-An-A-Co" machine was dismissed by most of the medical profession as a fraud.

In some ways, he fit right in with some of his millionaire neighbors in Pasadena, especially the contingent in Pasadena which was the American counterpart of the Fabian Socialists in England of the time. Two Fabianist authors, H.G. Wells and George Bernard Shaw, regularly communicated by letter with Sinclair in Pasadena. And Wilshire, who was Sinclair's neighbor, traveled to England constantly.

Others in Pasadena society who were part of the Sinclair group included Charles Chaplin, the "plant wizard" Luther Burbank, Mrs. Kate Crane-Gartz of the Crane plumbing fortune, Bobby Scripps of the newspaper chain, and land and oil heiress Alaine Barnsdall, whose name is perhaps best remembered today because of the park that carries it.

Sinclair owned several cottages in the 1500 block of Sunset Boulevard (long since torn down for a freeway). But he was close by the Pasadena socialists. He used to go walking with Henry Ford in the San Gabriel Mountains behind Pasadena; they would discuss politics and economics. Finally Sinclair realized that he wasn't getting anywhere with Ford. He reasoned that perhaps another millionaire, a socialist, could better convince Ford. So he asked King Gillette, the socialist razor king, to argue with the capitalist flivver king. Gillette was no more successful than Sinclair had been.

Of all his friends, aside from Charlie Chaplin, Wilshire was the closest. When Wilshire's gold mine was going badly, Sinclair gave him most of what he had left from the fortune he had made with *The Jungle*. He also encouraged other socialists to do so—but the gold mine went under anyway.

Sinclair made thousands and spent thousands—usually on his crusades. He published his own books in California because the New York publishers had proven fickle and unreliable. So books, magazines, pamphlets and whatnot issued forth from Sinclair's Pasadena post office box. Sinclair had far less trouble with his publishers overseas; he kept the same publisher in England for half a century. The Russians published millions of copies of Sinclair's works. But Sinclair did not always run his publishing business like a business. He distributed thousands of copies of *Flivver King* at his own expense to auto workers organizing in Detroit.

The group of millionaire socialists around Sinclair often came up with money for their crusades—but the financial dealings between Sinclair and Wilshire had been especially close. At one desperate point, Sinclair had offered to sell himself into indentured servitude to Wilshire for several years, for a certain amount of money. Wilshire declined the author's offer, but he lent and gave plenty of money to Sinclair over the years of their friendship.

Sinclair's name was closely connected, in quite a different way, with yet another of L.A.'s illustrious pioneers, General Harris Gray Otis, proprietor and editor of the *Los Angeles Times*. Sinclair and Otis had one of the city's most legendary feuds.

Back in 1882, according to David Halberstam's recent bestseller, *The Powers That Be,* General Otis was made an offer by the city's circulation czar that the general couldn't refuse. Harry Chandler, who controlled the circulation of most of the city's several dailies, struck a bargain with Otis, and the general's competitors simply ceased to have viable newspaper properties any more. The ambitious young Chandler then went to work as circulation manager for the *Times* and ascended the ladder of success even further by the simple device of becoming Otis's son-in-law. The following year, Southern Pacific gave L.A. its first rail link to the outside world, and the City of the Angels ceased to be a dusty little village of five thousand souls. Thus was the Chandler dynasty born.

The general died in 1917, the year after Sinclair settled in Pasadena. When in 1920 Sinclair published his book *The Brass Check,* much of his famed study of American journalism was about the general. In *The Brass Check* Sinclair repeated a story about Otis that Wilshire had told him. It seems that once, close to the turn of the century, Wilshire met the general on the street. Otis was being solicitous about a newspaper based on the utopian socialist ideas of Edward Bellamy, which Wilshire and others were publishing. In view of various editorials which had appeared in the *Times,* Wilshire was surprised that Otis was so concerned about the *Nationalist.*

"I see you people have got a weekly paper," the general said. Wilshire nodded in affirmation.

"Well now," said the general, "the *Times* has a new and modern printing plant. We would like very much to do that work for you. Suppose you give us a trial."

The *Nationalist* was being printed in the print shop of the old *Express*. Wilshire said he personally wouldn't object to its being printed at the *Times,* but he was sure that some of his associates would probably say that the general didn't treat their ideas fairly in the *Times.*

To this the general is supposed to have replied, "Oh, now, now, you don't mind a thing like that. Surely, now, you ought to understand a joke." Whereupon for the next several days the *Times* carried cordial editorials upon the ideas of Edward Bellamy's socialism. This went on for two or three weeks, but when the *Nationalist* kept on being printed at the *Express,* the general "shifted back to his old method of sneering and abuse," Sinclair reported.

If you get the impression that Sinclair was trying to say that the general was a venal and corrupt character, you are quite right. Sinclair's dislike of the general, however, was not based solely on something that had happened years ago to his friend, Wilshire. Shortly after settling in Pasadena in 1916, Sinclair had been invited, as a celebrity author, to give a lecture to one of the ladies' cultural clubs, "which," he noted, "pay celebrities to come and entertain them, and next to marrying a millionairess, this is the easiest way to get your living in Southern California." Sinclair was no more averse to making a buck than the next socialist, and when he made his appearance before the Friday Morning Club, he was a success. He scandalized and shocked the audience, as they wanted, but he also entertained. Everyone seemed quite happy with the arrangement.

Sinclair was not so well received, however, the next morning in the august pages of the *Los Angeles Times.*

The account of Sinclair's speech had been written by the general himself. The general's news account said the speech was "more-or-less brilliant quotations upholding anarchy, destruction, lawlessness, revolution, from the lips of an effeminate young man with a fatuous smile, a weak chin and a sloping forehead, talking in a false treble, and accusing them of leading selfish, self-indulgent lives." The *Times* story said that Sinclair had expressed his sympathy with dynamiters and murderers, and it added that "never before an audience of red-blooded men could Upton Sinclair have voiced his weak, pernicious, vicious doctrines. His naive, fatuous smile alone would have aroused their ire before he opened his vainglorious mouth. Let the fact remain that this slim, beflanneled example of perverted masculinity could and did get several hundred women to listen to him."

The general followed up this news account with editorials for the next several days demanding that Sinclair be incarcerated forthwith.

Not surprisingly, Sinclair wasn't very fond of the general either. "I have yet to meet a single person," he wrote in *The Brass Check*, "who does not despise and hate his *Times*. This paper, founded by Harrison Gray Otis, one of the most corrupt and most violent old men that ever appeared in American public life, has continued for thirty years to rave at every conceivable social reform, with complete disregard for truth, and with abusiveness which seems almost insane. It would seem better to turn loose a hundred thousand mad dogs in the streets of Los Angeles than to send out a hundred thousand copies of the *Times* every day."

The year the general died was a big one. The Russian Revolution had broken out toward the end of World War I, the czar and his family were in jail, and a socialist by the name of Kerensky was wondering what to do with them. (Kerensky, who was later overthrown by Lenin and his Bolsheviks, ended up living in Berkeley.) Sinclair sent him some advice. He suggested the czar and family be sent to Catalina Island, since this island off the coast of Los Angeles "is populated by sheep, the proper subject for autocracy." His idea was that Catalina should be made a "refuge for rulers abdicating or dethroned." Sinclair said his suggestion was made in order to boost the "wonderful outdoor climate and beautiful islands with wild goats running over them, and deep sea fishing, to be found" in Southern California. This sounded like a satire of the general's obsessive boosterism of Southern California, which Sinclair once described as a "smug and self-satisfied" community that is "a parasite upon the great industrial centers of other parts of America."

Wilshire read *The Brass Check* and warned its author that he'd never get away with publishing it. He urged Sinclair to get copies of it into the hands of socialists all over the country as fast as he could, and then have them hide their copies in their homes.

Sinclair took Wilshire's advice seriously. "It was an easy way to get rid of books," he later commented, "but a hard way to make money." The fact is that *The Brass Check* would eventually go through many printings, although Sinclair often had to connive to get the paper to print in on. He was convinced that this was no accident.

Sinclair wasn't much enamored of Los Angeles's other major publisher, William Randolph Hearst, either. He talked about the "daily cat and dog fight" between Hearst's *Examiner* and Otis's *Times* with obvious contempt for both papers. On the other hand, not so many years before, Sinclair had regarded the young Hearst as something of a messiah who might have led the country into the promised land if only he had made good on his ambition to be president. Furthermore, Sinclair wrote for the Hearst press. As late as 1923, he was writing a series in Hearst's *New York American,* which ran his stories with such sensational headlines as "Plutocracy Rules American Colleges,"

"U.S. Colleges Under Control of Morgan Gold," "Secret Societies Rule Yale," "Democracy is Gone," and "The Desperate Struggle for the World's Oil." Sinclair wrote on a variety of other subjects for Hearst, ranging from psychology to women's liberation.

Also in 1923, Sinclair was jailed in San Pedro during a "Wobbly" strike. He was arrested while speaking to seven hundred strikers. He stood on private property, and he had written permission from the owner to be there. He was reading the Declaration of Independence and the First Amendment to the Constitution. He was held incommunicado overnight—and out of the incident came the Southern California branch of the American Civil Liberties Union. Of all the things Sinclair accomplished in his life, he listed the founding of the Southland branch of the ACLU as one of the most important.

The Brass Check was received with accolades all over the world. The notorious cynic and wit H.L. Mencken wrote of the book to Sinclair: "I find nothing that seems to me to be exaggerated. On the contrary, you have, in many ways, much understated your case." But Mencken could not go along with Sinclair's suggestion that socialism was the answer. "To hell with socialism," he said. "The longer I live, the more I am convinced that the common people are doomed to be diddled forever. You are fighting a vain fight. But you must be having lots of fun."

Mencken and Sinclair carried on an exchange of their views over the years, and Mencken even came and visited Sinclair in Pasadena. They argued about booze and Jack London. Mencken was, of course, firmly committed to booze. Sinclair was a prohibitionist—it's been suggested more than once that the sight of his drunken father made him that way.

Part of the reason *The Jungle* had been such a success was because London had trumpeted its cause. When they met, however, London told Sinclair about various alcoholic and hashish debauches he had wit-nessed. At the same time, London was getting drunker and drunker as they talked. Sinclair was shocked and upset. To his way of thinking, London had ruined himself with drink. But Mencken argued that had it not been for booze, London probably wouldn't have been a great writer.

Certainly Sinclair's presence in Southern California added to the area's intellectual atmosphere. Not long after Sinclair had settled down in Pasadena, George Bernard Shaw wrote to him, saying, "I hear about all sorts of interesting people being at Pasadena, which I suppose is due to your having settled there (for six months as usual, eh?). If I ever get to the States I will try to find where Pasadena is."

Sinclair also carried on a lengthy correspondence during his early days in Pasadena with a young English writer named Winston Churchill. And there was always considerable correspondence between Sinclair and Sinclair Lewis. When Lewis came and visited Upton Sinclair in Pasadena, the younger man went way out of his way to arrive sober—which was not necessarily his most natural state.

Both Eugene Debs and Clarence Darrow, the famed socialist and the crusading lawyer, respectively, were visitors in Pasadena. Later, of course, Albert Einstein, when he was at the nearby California Institute of Technology, spent long hours with Sinclair. Both were amateur violinists, and they liked to get together in Sinclair's backyard and drag horsehair over cat gut.

Then there was correspondence from the great playwright Eugene O'Neill, who told Sinclair how much he had been affected by *The Jungle* and how he was thinking of moving out to California soon. Thomas Mann and Sinclair had corresponded even before Mann, forced to flee Germany, ended up in exile in Los Angeles.

When all the letters, manuscripts and papers Sinclair had accumulated over a lifetime were moved from his last home in the Southland, there were eight tons of material. Sinclair lived in his Monrovia home (which is now an unmarked national monument at 464 N. Myrtle) until the early '6os. He offered his papers to the Huntington in San Marino, but at the time the famed museum said it wasn't interested. Finally, the Sinclair collection went to the Lilly Library at Indiana University.

Sinclair replied to almost anybody's letters. He wrote hundreds of letter giving advice on everything from sex to diet and politics. He was known as a soft touch for any young writer who wanted an opinion from a famous author. But toward the end of the '20s, there was just getting to be too much correspondence; he wasn't getting his own work done.

So in 1927, the Sinclairs moved to a modest house in Long Beach. It is still there, at 10 58th Place. According to John Ahouse, who is not only the editor of *Uppie Speaks,* but is also the special collections librarian at Long Beach State University, Sinclair's Long Beach period was especially productive. Ahouse points out that he produced such classics during his Long Beach period as *Oil!, Boston, Money Writes* and *Mental Radio.*

Sinclair's wife, Mary Craig, had a passion for real estate speculation, like the rest of Southern California in the '20s, and she owned a couple of parcels of land on Signal Hill in Long Beach. The discovery of oil there put her square in the middle of the Signal Hill oil boom, which was one of the biggest in the nation at the time. She made a few thousand dollars from her speculation. More important, Sinclair got the raw material for *Oil!* He watched with fascination as the drama of the oil boom unfolded; soon he was taking notes and interviewing everyone. He wrote his yarn against a backdrop of wheeling and dealing, bribery and corruption. "A picture of civilization in Southern California," he said. All of Sinclair's favorite subjects are to be found in *Oil!* — there are evangelists and college presidents and newspaper publishers. The book

is also the most convincing of Sinclair's novels from a psychological as well as a political standpoint – and after *The Jungle,* critics usually rate it as his best work.

During the Long Beach period, Mary Craig also drew Sinclair's prodigious attention to psychic phenomena – he was so convinced that she had ESP that he wrote a book called *Mental Radio.* The book drew the attention of the famed pioneer psychic researcher J.B. Rhine of Duke University. But Sinclair's old friend Bertrand Russell refused to write an introduction to the book, flatly dismissing ESP. Albert Einstein, on the other hand, did do an introduction to the German edition.

Mental Radio produced correspondence from Sir Arthur Conan Doyle, creator of Sherlock Holmes, in 1929. Doyle, who had said he regarded Sinclair as "one of the greatest novelists in the world, the Zola of America," shared Sinclair's interest in ESP. One of his letters to Sinclair said that he was impressed with Sinclair's famous attack on organized religion, *Profits of Religion.* But Doyle added: "Don't run down Spiritualism. It is the one solid patch in the whole quagmire of religion. Of course there are frauds, quacks, though that has been exaggerated."

The Long Beach period came to an end in 1931 because Sinclair was getting involved in Hollywood studio work. It was the time of the Great Depression, and Sinclair purchased a genuine Beverly Hills mansion at 614 N. Arden Drive: it was cheap, he pointed out, because there was no market then for big houses. Sinclair was doing very well financially – so much so that his old friend Charlie Chaplin got him both financially and creatively involved with the great Russian film director Sergei Eisenstein. Eisenstein spent several months and a pile of Sinclair's money working on his *Thunder over Mexico.*

The late Sol Lesser, who produced such films as *Stagedoor Canteen, Our Town, The Red House* and *Kon-Tiki,* was deeply involved with Sinclair on *Thun-*

der over Mexico. Eventually, however, Sinclair sold the rights of the film to Stalin, just to try and recoup a fraction of what he had lost on it, and started becoming even more anti-Communist than he had under Mary Craig's promptings.

Politics was ultimately to direct Sinclair's efforts away from the studios. The Depression was deepening. Sinclair had already taken out his typewriter and knocked off a couple of books telling what he would do about the country's financial problems—*I, Candidate for Governor,* and *How I Ended Poverty: A True Story of the Future.* They were novels, but among the people they impressed was a contingent of Democrats in Santa Monica, including the owner of one of that town's biggest hotels. They like his ideas about what to do, and kept urging him to run for governor as a Democrat, not a Socialist.

So while living in the Beverly Hills mansion, Sinclair changed his voting registration from Socialist to Democratic. He pointed out that he had been raised a Democrat; in fact his great-grandfather, Commodore Arthur Sinclair, had been one of the original founders of the Democratic party. But Sinclair had become disillusioned with the Democratic party during his youth in New York City, as he watched how Tammany Hall was ruining Gotham.

Unlike the communists and his former socialist comrades, Sinclair had made a discovery about California. "There is little working-class mentality." Talking about the Golden State's inhabitants, he observed: "They were middle-class in their thoughts and feelings, and even the most hopeless among them were certain their children were going to get an education and rise in the world."

Thus it was out of a book, a book that was really only fiction, that Sinclair's EPIC movement—End Poverty in California—was born. The EPIC plan became a giant grassroots movement such as California has not seen since. There were EPIC clubs, EPIC theatres and an EPIC newspaper, which had a daily circulation of two million at one point in Sinclair's campaign.

EPIC forced a major realignment of both the Democratic and Republican parties in California. Despite the fact that the Republican Frank Merriam won against Sinclair in November, the Democratic party went on to become the majority party; before EPIC almost all of the governors had been Republicans, and so had been most of the voters.

The campaign against Sinclair was also one of the most vicious smear jobs in political history. It also had the dubious distinction of being the first time advertising men were hired to run a candidacy. Republican Frank Merriam's campaign was managed by the firm of Lord & Thomas, financed by a cabal of powerful California interests, and led by Sinclair's old nemesis, the *Los Angeles Times.*

Sinclair told the story afterwards in his book, *I, Candidate for Governor: And How I Got Licked.* And David Halberstam's *The Powers That Be* describes a young *New York Times* reporter, Turner Catledge, who had come to California in 1934 with an assignment to find out about what was happening to the Sinclair candidacy. Catledge picked up the *Los Angeles Times* but could find no mention of where he might go and listen to Sinclair. *The Los Angeles Times* didn't run that kind of information about Sinclair. Instead there was simply a story saying that Sinclair was attacking the Bible and was un-Christian.

Later Catledge went to dinner with Kyle Palmer, the political correspondent and king-maker of California politics for the *Los Angeles Times.* Palmer told Catledge to forget "that kind of crap that you have in New York of being obliged to print both sides. We're going to beat this son of a bitch Sinclair any way we can. We're going to kill him."

Halberstam's book goes on to describe some things Catledge was not aware of when he had dinner with Palmer. The *Los Angeles Times* had lent Palmer to Louis B. Mayer, the movie mogul, who had decided to use the studios in any way he could to stop Sinclair. Newsreels were faked, and the Depression-packed movie houses up and down the state were required by the studios to run them—not as political advertising but as legitimate news. In one of those newsreels, for instance, there was a wild-looking, bearded Russian anarchist telling the camera crew that he was going to vote for Sinclair because "His system vorked vell in Russia, vy can't it vork here?" Other newsreels showed hordes of unemployed laborers sitting at the California borders, waiting to come and get Sinclair's welfare when he won the governorship. The only problem is that the "unemployed" were movie extras!

Uppie Speaks publisher Hahn claims that the *Los Angeles Times* employed one gentleman full-time in a secret room in the *Times* building. His job was to go through all of Sinclair's books and find juicy quotes on subjects ranging from free love to religion. These quotes were then run, wildly out of context, in big black borders on the front page. The amazing thing, Hahn says, is that despite the smear job, Sinclair still got forty-five percent of the vote in the general election.

Sinclair has been portrayed as some sort of hedonistic, devilish creature when in truth he was very much a Puritan. If anything, some of his radical friends found Sinclair just too much of a saint, a fanatic on "clean" living. It was also obvious to a lot of people that Sinclair directed his sexual energies into his work, for there had to be some explanation for the incredible amounts of work he accomplished.

There was something out of sorts in Sinclair's sexual makeup. His first marriage had foundered on his wife's infidelity. She actively pursued and believed in the free-love ideas popular at the time. It then seems as if there was almost no physical passion at all in his second marriage. Mary Craig married Sinclair only after long agonizing between Sinclair and his old Carmel poet friend George Sterling. In 1928 in Long Beach, Sinclair actually published some of Sterling's love sonnets to Mary Craig.

One can see his puritanical sensibilities in this shocked description, in *The Brass Check,* of a certain "gorgeous and expensive leisure-class hotel" in Pasadena. Sinclair wrote with obvious horror about "the elderly ladies of fashion who were putting paint on their cheeks, and cutting their dresses halfway down their backs, and making open efforts to seduce" the young men on the premises. He complained that young matrons "disappeared for trips into the mountain canyons nearby" with members of the opposite sex. Then there was "the married lady of great wealth who had been in several scandals, who caroused all night with half a dozen soldiers and sailors, supplying them all with all the liquor they wanted in spite of the law, and who finally was asked to leave the hotel—not because of this carousing but because she failed to pay the liquor bill."

At the same time Sinclair was a leading exponent of women's rights—and a great friend and ally of pioneer feminist Margaret Sanger. But he carried on about the treachery of "fast women" with all the righteous indignation of an old-fashioned Episcopalian minister. At one point he proclaimed: "Take it from me, there is no possibility of happiness in sex life—under our present social system, at any rate—except to find a decent girl who will be true and to whom it's worth being true." The problem with these lofty sentiments, of course, is that one's strong impression is that Sinclair and his second wife eschewed sex.

And Sinclair's first wife, Meta, had offered this analysis of Sinclair: "He is conservative by instinct and a radical by choice. Mr. Sinclair is an essential monogamist, without having any of the qualities which an essential monogamist ought to possess."

During the Second World War, Sinclair began his immensely popular Lanny Budd series, and he spent a lot of time nursing his ailing wife as well. They had moved to the pleasant house on Myrtle in Monrovia. Finally, because of the smog, Sinclair and his wife moved away for a while to Arizona. But finally they returned to California, where Mary Craig died in 1961.

Sinclair subsequently married May Hard Willis and outlived her. He died at ninety years of age in a New Jersey nursing home, one year after being honored by President Lyndon Baines Johnson during the signing of a new meat packing reform bill.

Was Sinclair a great writer? *Uppie Speaks* editor John Ahouse says he frequently argues with Robert O. Hahn, the newsletter's publisher, over just this issue. Ahouse is willing to admit that Sinclair's prose did not always "offer the literary substance academic English departments are looking for." Ahouse says that Sinclair becomes really intriguing only when you're looking at his life as a whole, and not judging him by any single piece of writing. "You have to become aware of the issues he was fighting for" and then "his sense of personal integrity begins to communicate itself." Hahn, on the other hand, thinks that English departments who refuse to take Sinclair seriously do so simply because they are "snobs."

Ahouse says he does not find it surprising at all that Sinclair's popularity has slipped in his own country while it has maintained itself in some European countries. The idea of "fiction put to the service of an idea" is a less popular notion in our country than in other countries, he says.

Ahouse doesn't downgrade Sinclair's importance, of course. In fact, he is working hard at building up Long Beach State University's special collection on Sinclair. Still, he says, "when the smoke clears, his place will perhaps have been more in social history than purely literature." Hahn, on the other hand, derides the notion that one can study literature without connecting it with history, or that one can know history without knowing the literature of the period. Also, literature and history have to arise in a place—the place helps define both. Los Angeles helped give Sinclair to the world.

NINE

Can Bohemia Thrive Here Once Again?

Williiam Koshland poked dubiously at his poached eggs and tried to say something nice about Los Angeles as he looked at the Cadillacs and Ferraris and fashionplate people going by the window of the Beverly-Wilshire Hotel coffee shop. It wasn't easy. I tried to assure him that there was more to Los Angeles than Beverly Hills. We were talking about Thomas Mann's period in Los Angeles, when he wrote *Doctor Faustus*. Koshland was laughing at my description of Michael Mann, son of the German novelist, who used to drink a gallon of cheap red wine every night in my parents' West Los Angeles home.

Koshland is Editor Emeritus of Alfred A. Knopf, Inc. He was also the editor of the *Doctor Faustus* manuscript in the 1940s and as a result got to know the Mann family well. Mann's nephew, Klaus H. Pringsheim, wrote to the *Los Angeles Herald Examiner* complaining about my having written of Michael's drinking cheap red California wine. Michael drank "fairly respectable French reds," Pringsheim insisted.

Koshland, however, verified my memory of Michael's endless bottles of a cheap California wine. Koshland said that he met Michael one time in an airport and that Michael was "drinking that same bottle of California red wine." Koshland said that this was shortly after Thomas Mann had died. Michael had come to New York to sell his father's lifetime correspondence, and Koshland told him he shouldn't just put them on the auction block to the highest bidder. Koshland argued that Knopf should publish the Mann letters since Knopf had been Mann's faithful American publisher for so many years. Michael took another drink and failed to heed Koshland's advice.

Koshland was a little less jovial—he had complimented me highly on my Mann piece—when we got to talking about his own publishing firm, which he joined back in 1931. He denied that Knopf had lost its commitment to literature as a result of becoming part of a large conglomerate rather than remaining a family-owned firm. He could probably tell that I wasn't entirely convinced, but we were soon talking about Los Angeles, which he admitted he didn't know well; the coming apocalypse, which is a perennially popular topic around here; and the Holocaust, the subject about which Mann had written so brilliantly in *Doctor Faustus*.

It was not long after my meeting with Koshland that the year 1980 began, and the decade dawned with some furious storms. My series of articles examining Los Angeles and her great writers was leading me to a conclusion with which I was not very comfortable. This realization came to me one night as all around me L.A. seemed to be disintegrating in mud slides, rain and yet more rain. I was one of the lucky ones. The roof of my Silverlake apartment had only sprung a minor leak. Normally the view from my second-story apartment shows me all of Hollywood, including the Griffith Park Observatory. But that night the rain was falling so hard I wondered if I was back in London. Suddenly an unholy amount of lightning, lightning such as I had rarely seen in Los Angeles, flashed awesomely and the roof literally rolled from the thunder. I laughed at the realization that in Los Angeles one's thoughts turn to apocalypse when it rains a little harder than usual. Of course there was all the inevitable bad news on the international scene. Worse, the newspapers had been full for the last several months of articles talking about The Big Earthquake, and about how the San Andreas fault was moving this way and that, so that almost everyone agreed that the Big One—the Really Big One—was on the way. You couldn't see all of Hollywood that night and maybe the big earthquake or these rains or an atomic war was about to wipe out Los Angeles, but at the moment the sound of the rain was nice. It had turned the lights of Hollywood into a diffused, rain-smeared image of warm, shimmering colors. The outlines of the city were visible, and yes they could have been on the set of a futuristic city before the Apocalypse. Could such a place produce valid literature? Would it be around long enough to do so?

Then one of the lightning bolts hit only a few feet away, in the empty lot across the street. I saw at close range the cold, death-like glow from that lightning, and it sobered me even more than had the sight of suicides, car-crash fatalities and other such things I had seen during my years on police beat. Perhaps what was terrifying was that this wasn't a man-made killer, that lightning bolt. I felt as if I had seen death close-up. The color of the electricity on the lot was brilliant and cold.

All of the four great literary works of the twentieth century that Los Angeles had a hand in were works of apocalyptical vision. They had been written during the Depression and the Second World War, but the fact is that they had been produced at least in part because of Los Angeles. The four works were also quite dissimilar. *Doctor Faustus,* Mann's novel of gloom and doom, was inspired not only by what was going on in his homeland, but also by the proximity in L.A. of his neighbor and acquaintance, Arnold Schoenberg, grandaddy of avant-garde music.

Malcolm Lowry's *Under the Volcano* owed a lot to Los Angeles, even though he hated the place. There was the cinematic influence of Hollywood. Also, he met his future wife, who almost co-authored *Under the Volcano,* in Los Angeles. And it appears that he worked on the manuscript here.

To go on with these four horsemen of the apocalypse, Nathanael West wrote his famed *The Day of the Locust* about actual people and places of Hollywood. Then, towards the end of the Second World War, a countryman of Lowry's, Aldous Huxley, wrote the ultimate apocalyptical vision of Los Angeles. In his novel, *Ape & Essence,* Huxley visualized Los Angeles after the atomic annihilation of the world. Oddly enough, unlike other great expatriate writers, Huxley did not abandon L.A. as soon as the war in Europe was over. He adopted L.A. as his home.

Why, I wondered, has L.A. produced so much gloom and doom? Is it because it truly is the City of the Future?

This project of mine, writing about writers and a city, dates back to my childhood love of the California Bohemian movement, the grandfather of which was Mark Twain in San Francisco. Most of the writers I ever loved after that could be counted among the ranks of the Bohemians. Since a big part of the tradition of the Bohemian writers was journalistic, I went to work on newspapers when I was nineteen years old.

One lazy afternoon in the late '60s, Scott Newhall, who was the editor of the *Newhall Signal* where I was then employed, as well as the editor of the *San Francisco Chronicle* where I'd later be employed, expounded at great length on his views of newspapers and literature. Newhall said newspapermen—real ones, that is—were called to the profession in the way other were called to the priesthood. Of course, as editor of the *San Francisco Chronicle,* Newhall was right in touch with the Bohemian tradition, for the *Chronicle* had been a part of that tradition during its long history. Today I wonder if the present editor of the *Chronicle,* which has lost most of its Bohemian flavor since Newhall left it, would believe that journalism should be practiced as a kind of daily literature.

But when, more than a decade later, I walked in to see Dick Adler, at that time the editor of the *Los Angeles Herald Examiner's* Sunday magazine section, I felt as if Bohemia had not entirely disappeared. I was confronted with a burly, balding, bearded gentleman—which, incidentally, is not a bad description of me, either. Adler told me that he couldn't pay well, so I ought to have fun and write stories I cared about, stories that would possibly be significant. I didn't have to try and get excited about making a list of the ten best boutiques in Encino, or where to get your poodles clipped in Burbank, or whatever kind of nonsense excites trendy magazine editors these days.

Thus I began my literary chores by writing about the house that Finn Frolich built in Hollywood's La

Vista Court, which was visible proof of this Bohemian influence. The existence of the Jack London House—for in part Frolich had dedicated the place to his old sailing companion—had never been revealed in print.

It is possible that London stayed in a small shack around which Frolich built his sculpture studio later. Most certainly George Sterling, the poet who single-handedly kept the Bohemian movement thriving after the turn of the century, spent time in London House, as evidenced by his inscription to Frolich, which remains in the house.

It intrigued me that the name of George Sterling seemed to show up whenever an important California writer from his time was mentioned. It was Sterling's original promotion of Robinson Jeffers, for example, that launched the latter's career as a poet. It was also Sterling who convinced Upton Sinclair—who had become famous in 1906 with his sensational exposé of the meat-packing industry, *The Jungle*—to come to California.

The writers who gathered around Sterling nurtured philosophical positions that clashed and connected in strange ways. Take for example three of Sterling's good friends: Upton Sinclair, Jack London and Robinson Jeffers. London and Jeffers, who otherwise made an odd couple, had both been mightily influenced by the German philosopher Nietzsche. Jeffers, however, was staunchly conservative in politics and economics. Sterling, Sinclair and London, on the other hand, were militant socialists. In the case of London, his inability to reconcile his Nietzsche and his Marx drove him to drink. Their Bohemianism was eclectic, but it was highly rebellious and produced some of this country's most original poetry and prose.

In the post-war years the Bohemians became part of history. They were replaced by the beatniks, who congregated in coffeehouses in Venice and in old L.A. neighborhoods like Echo Park. Yet interestingly enough, the thread that links the Bohemians and the Beats can be found in an area south of downtown, called Watts.

One of the most important of the nation's black writers grew up here at the turn of the century. In his classic work called *Anyplace But Here*, Arna Bontemps went back to his childhood memories of the sweetness as well as the problems of Watts. What he was doing was tracing the evolution of black ghettoes, and Watts became his archetypical "Mudtown" (his name for northern ghetto communities).

Bontemps originally was shipped to Watts by his father after his mother died in his native Louisiana. He grew up and went to school in Watts and worked at the post office at night. But after college he went to Harlem, where he teamed up with Langston Hughes to help create the Harlem Renaissance of the 1920s.

In *Anyplace But Here* Bontemps wrote of Watts with great love. He wrote with special fondness of Jelly Roll Morton and his coterie of New Orleans jazz greats whose heyday was in Los Angeles during the '30s. Bontemps told of how, before the Second World War, "Los Angeles in legend became 'paradise west' to Negroes still languishing in Egyptland of the South."

In a book of letters between Bontemps and Hughes, editor Charles H. Nichols makes the point that these two writers grew out of the American tradition of Whitman and Twain. He goes on to say, "The Beat writers owed even more than they acknowledge to writers like Hughes and Bontemps." Mentioning Jack Kerouac and Norman Mailer, he contends that these writers even owed the word "beat" to blacks. "Beat is a word derived from the language of lower-class Negroes, meaning 'poor, down-and-out, dead-beat, on the bum, sad, sleeping in the subways,'" Nichols declares.

Certainly one of the obvious features of the L.A. coffeehouse scene of the 1950s and '60s was the mixing of black and white, often through the medium of music. *The Air-Conditioned Nightmare* by Henry Miller was the bible of the disaffected, who played chess and listened to jazz. But after Kennedy's assassination in 1963, the civil rights and anti-war protests came hand in glove, and what had been a primarily spiritual and cultural protest became political.

At the same time, printing technology had made giant strides forward as the result of cold type and offset printing. Out of the coffeehouse scenes of Los Angeles and San Francisco poured "alternative" newspapers and a burgeoning small press movement. Although New York is supposed to be the nation's literary capital, the small press movement flourished on the West Coast. Today many of the nation's small independent literary publishers are in California.

My friend William Koshland, the Knopf editor, is connected with one of the last New York publishing houses that continues to make a commitment to good writing. It's a battle. There are very few people like him left to fight.

Joseph Simon is one of the surviving partners of Ward Ritchie, the old-line small California press, now defunct, that was based in Pasadena. Ward Ritchie published the poetry of Robinson Jeffers as far back as the 1930s. Today Simon publishes limited editions of Jonathan Swift, Jack London and other greats, from his trailer in Malibu. He surveyed the books coming from New York publishing houses and decided that they were all catchy-sounding, promising and titillating, but that in the process of marketing books with titles like *How to Have Sex Alone and Still Enjoy It With Somebody Else,* no one was paying any attention to the contents. Books from New York publishers are designed to sell, not to be read, he concluded. Simon tells the parable of the man who purchased all the tins of sardines on sale at a particular grocery store because they were so cheap. As the story goes, the man turned around and sold the sardines to various other people, who were soon calling him back to complain about how rotten the sardines were. When the entrepreneur went back to the grocery store to complain, the manager looked at him sternly and asked

him what his purpose had been in buying the sardines. You see, said the grocer, those were buying-and-selling sardines, not eating sardines. Similarly, says Simon, New York publishers have degraded literature. He points out that, for years, the writers who have fueled New York's publishing industry have made their home on the West Coast—not just great writers but many very good ones as well. Simon is hoping that there will be a renaissance of print, and that it will come from the West.

Simon takes the optimistic side in the old debate about whether or not we are headed into a new electronic Dark Ages in which the ability to read, and hence the ability to think and evaluate, will be lost. Some critics have pointed an especially accusing finger at Los Angeles for its role in the advent of electronic darkness. But this book has, I hope, shown some sort of synthesis, some merging that occurred in Los Angeles, that has added to the written word all over the world.

Los Angeles's literary tradition was begun by the California Bohemians. Then, by various circumstances of history, the city also played host to some of the refugee artists from the European Holocaust. And some of the refugee writers from the eastern part of the country came, too—writers such as Faulkner, Fitzgerald, West and Parker who couldn't make a living during the Depression anywhere else but in Hollywood. It is clear that the Holocaust—which the Depression was a part of—was of necessity reflected in the writing that emerged from Los Angeles during that period. And the ground for some of that writing had been broken by the Bohemians at the turn of the century.

Today in New York you will find lots of critics who have wrongly assumed that Los Angeles has no literary traditions to draw on, save those grafted onto it by Hollywood. This is because New York thinks it all has to happen in Gotham. But this is not true. When one understands the fullness of the literary tradition that has emerged and will continue to emerge in Los Angeles, one sees that the City of the Angels has had an intellectual and literary life of distinctive merit and great potential.

True, since the Second World War, the Beat scene has come and gone. And there seem to have been no more Mark Twains anywhere in the nation, on the west or the east coasts. Some might make the argument that Kate Braverman and Joan Didion are contemporary Bohemians. Or how about Charles Bukowski? Perhaps. But none of these names has shown the outsize talent, or the social consciousness, that the really great writers in Los Angeles had in abundance. To my tired old eyes, the contemporary names are too self-absorbed, and offer no larger world-view. Various observers have told me I really should be more open to the modern writers, so I have tried. I have thumbed through their books and poems, and I've admired how they put their words together. But their words don't dance off the page the way Twain's or London's did. Many people tell me that a lot of writers are about to happen soon who will make me change my tune. This movement or that person is going to have a profound effect first on L.A. and then on the world. My friend, writer and editor Dorothy Schuler, has emphatically insisted, for example, that there is a whole generation of women writers about to burst on the scene, people who will truly carry on the tradition. It would be nice to think that perhaps she is not being overly optimistic.

SUGGESTED BIBLIOGRAPHY

BIOGRAPHIES, STUDIES AND MEMOIRS OF SPECIAL NOTE

Bennett, Melba Berry. *The Stone Mason of Tor House: Life and Work of Robinson Jeffers.* Ward Ritchie, 1966.

Brophy, Robert. *Robinson Jeffers: Myth, Ritual and Symbol in his Poems.* The Press of Case Western Reserve University, 1973.

Cross, Richard. *Malcolm Lowry: A Preface to His Fiction.* University of Chicago Press, 1980.

Day, Douglas. *Malcolm Lowry.* Oxford University Press, 1973.

Epstein, Perle. *The Private Labyrinth of Malcolm Lowry.* Holt, Rinehart, and Winston, 1969.

Hamilton, Nigel. *The Brothers Mann: The Lives of Heinrich and Thomas Mann.* Martin Secker & Warburg, 1978.

Harris, Leon. *Upton Sinclair: An American Rebel.* T.Y. Crowell, 1975.

Heller, Erich. *The Ironic German: A Study of Thomas Mann.* Little, Brown & Company, 1958.

Keats, John. *You Might As Well Live: The Life and Times of Dorothy Parker.* Simon and Schuster, 1970.

Light, James F. *Nathanael West: An Interpretative Study.* Northwestern University Press, 1971.

Mann, Katia. *Unwritten Memories.* Alfred A. Knopf, 1975.

Mann, Thomas. *The Story of a Novel: The Genesis of Doctor Faustus.* Alfred A. Knopf, 1961.

Martin, Jay. *Nathanael West: The Art of His Life.* Farrar, Straus & Giroux, 1970.

Martin, Jay. *Always Merry and Bright: The Life of Henry Miller.* Capra Press, 1978.

Powell, Lawrence Clark. *Robinson Jeffers: The Man & His Work.* Primavera Press, 1934.

Sinclair, Upton. *Autobiography of Upton Sinclair.* Harcourt Brace & World, 1962.

Stone, Irving. *Jack London: Sailor on Horseback.* Doubleday & Company, 1977.

BOOKS OF CORRESPONDENCE

Steinbeck: A Life in Letters. Viking Press, 1975.
The Selected Letters of Malcolm Lowry. J.B. Lippincott, 1965.
Arnold Schoenberg Letters. Faber and Faber, 1964.
Letters of Thomas Mann. Alfred A. Knopf, 1970.
The Selected Letters of Robinson Jeffers. John Hopkins Press, 1968.

BOOKS OF GENERAL INTEREST

Dardis, Tom. *Some Time in the Sun.* Charles Scribner's Sons, 1976.

Walker, Franklin. *A Literary History of Southern California.* University of California Press, 1950.

Walker, Franklin. *The Seacoast of Bohemia.* Peregrine Smith, 1973.

ADDITIONAL NOTES

Much of the material in *Literary L.A.* was drawn from limited-edition books and from newspaper and magazine articles in special collections not easily available to the general public, as well as from the better-known biographies and collected letters of the different writers. In addition, the author conducted interviews with people who knew these writers, or who have become experts on their lives and works. Special mention should also be made of a series of articles by Lawrence Clark Powell which appeared in *Westways* magazine, called "California Classics Reread." Two on-going publications deserve special mention. *The Robinson Jeffers Newsletter* is published by the library at Occidental College, and *The Upton Sinclair Quarterly* is available from 3939 Glenridge Drive, Sherman Oaks, Calif. 91423.

INDEX